A MODEL CHURCH

A MODEL CHURCH

by
Ryder Kumar

Expository Messages From the Book of Philippians

A MODEL CHURCH
by Ryder Kumar

ISBN : 978-0-692-80128-4

Copyright © Ryder Kumar

First Edition 2016

All rights reserved.
No part of this publication may be reproduced in any form by any means, including those yet to be rewritten or changed, without permission in writing from the author. Scripture quotations, unless otherwise stated, are taken from the
ENGLISH STANDARD VERSION (2001) Bible®

Published by
10580 Tamarack Ave
Pacoima. CA 91331 U.S.A.
Phone : +91 970 122 1669 | +1 818 357 2330

Printed in India by
EL Printers, Hyderabad
Email : elprinters@gmail.com

A Tribute

I am profoundly impacted by the sacrificial services of my father, Dodda Abraham who brought great interest at a very early age in my life and introduced to the greatest book the Bible which has become my life's companion. I will never forget the day when he sat by me and taught scriptures. He took me to Sunday School and mentored me until the day he was called to glory. Hebrews 11:4 though he is dead, he still speaks.

Acknowledgments:

I am grateful to God for Flory Kumar, my wife who faithfully prayed, selflessly supported me and undertook to do the publication of this book. I am indebted to my son, Abraham Kumar a CTO at Contemporary Services Corporation and CEO of Protatech, stood by me during most difficult times of life and encouraged me in different ways which enabled me to preach the sermons on the book of Philippians. I am thankful for a friend like Paul Brown, Senior Pastor of The Bridge Bible Fellowship under whom I learnt what it means to preach passionately. His secretary, Carrie Carmichael has diligently done the editing of this book, whose contribution is never to be forgotten.

Contents:

1.	The Lord Uses People to Establish a Local Church	13
2.	True Christians Have a Significant Relationship...	25
3.	God is the Source	31
4.	Integral Connections within believers	41
5.	Bound by Inseparable Ties	50
6.	Preparing for the Day of Christ	54
7.	Advancement of the Gospel in the Midst...	65
8.	Examine Your Motives in Preaching the Gospel	76
9.	Marks of a Positive Life	84
10.	Features of Your Life on Earth	95
11.	Manner of a Life that is Worthy of the Gospel	104
12.	Appeal for Unity - Part I	112
13.	Appeal for Unity - Part II	121
14.	Have the Mind of Christ	129
15.	Exaltation Comes from God	137
16.	Work Out Your Own Salvation	145
17.	Life Designed by God for His Child	155
18.	Make Your Sacrifice with Joy	162
19.	People with a Profound Testimony	172
20.	A Profound Testimony Requires An Action Oriented Relationship	181
21.	Beware for Your Safety	190
22.	A Proper Perspective of Gain and Loss	196
23.	Christ has Made You His Own	207
24.	Are You Stagnant or Straining Forward?	215
25.	What is the Pattern for Your Walk on Earth?	223
26.	Exhortation to Admonish	230
27.	Practice What You Have Learned	237
28.	Are You Content?	242
29.	Partnership with God's People	247
30.	Final Words to Radiate God's Glory	257

Foreword

The late J. Vernon Mcgee commented that a preacher should endeavor to teach by "placing the cookies on the lower shelf," meaning that we should make the truth easily understandable. Ryder Kumar has attempted to do just that in his devotional commentary on Philippians. The combination of a pastor's heart, a missionary's zeal for the lost, and a scholar's mind come together to fashion a study in God's Word that both teaches the mind but also warms and encourages the heart. Ryder Kumar's years as a pastor is reflected in the chapter by chapter analysis of Paul's tender Book of Philippians. Each chapter is full of encouraging gems as well as Biblical insight.

I am pleased to see this work placed in the hands of our lay people, students of seminaries and colleges to help achieve a better understanding of this Apostolic letter, and to find rich encouragement for daily living. The church in America and in other parts of the world will be enriched by this fresh approach at the study of God's Word.

Dr. Alex Montoya
Associate Professor,
The Master's Seminary
Sun Valley, California

Chapter 1

The Lord Uses People to Establish a Local Church

Introduction: We are living in a day when the understanding of the church has become more complex than ever. For some it is a socio-religious gathering. For some it is a sort of spiritual entertainment. For some it is a place for rituals and religious activities for self-satisfaction. For some it is a denomination. But the church is none of these.

Many people have a distorted meaning of the "church." While some think it is "a building," others think it is a service. At the outset, we want to have a clear understanding of the "church." The Greek word, "ekklisia" means assembly or congregation or church. This refers to either the whole body of Christ or a local assembly of believers.

The first time the word appears in Scripture is in Matthew 16:18. The church in the Bible is not a building or a denomination but people. For by one Spirit we were all baptized into one body, whether Jews or Greeks, whether slave or free and we were all made to drink from one Spirit (1 Cor. 12:13). This body is the body of Christ. And He put all things in subjection under His feet, and gave Him as head over all things to the church, which is His body, the fullness of Him who fills all in all (Eph. 1:22-23). As the body has many members (1 Cor. 12:14).

The Lord Uses People to Establish a Local Church

So also Christ's body has many members. Now, which member do you think is important in the body? Is it a nose or hand or leg or some other member? Is not every member important? In the same way, every member in the Body of Christ is important. How do we become members of this body? Here we have the answer in the Scriptures: ...And the Lord was adding to their number day by day those who were being saved (Acts 2:47).

The Bible talks about the Church that is invisible which is a universal church and the visible church which is a local church. God uses His people to establish a local church. In this commentary on the book of Philippians, we will learn more about the church, but first, we will look at the fact that "God Uses People to Establish a Local Church."

One day the church will be caught up in other words raptured. People who are baptized into this body are going to be there in eternity with God. John Wesley once was much troubled in regard to the disposition of various sects, and the chances of each in reference to future happiness or punishment. A dream one night transported him in its uncertain wanderings to the gates of hell. "Are there any Roman Catholics here?" asked thoughtful Wesley. "Yes," was the reply. "Any Presbyterians?" "Yes," was again the answer. "Any Congregationalists?" "Yes" "Any Methodists?" by way of a clincher, asked the pious Wesley. "Yes" was the answer, to his great indignation. In the mystic way of dreams, there was a sudden transition, and he stood at the gates of heaven. Improving his opportunity, he again inquired, "Are there any Roman Catholics here?" "No," he replied. "Any Presbyterians?" "No" "Any congregationalists?" "No" "Well, then" he asked, lost in wonder, "who are they inside?" "Christians!" was the jubilant answer.

Now some might have this question, "Who is a Christian?" Is it that a person who professes to be a Christian is, in fact, a Christian? Or is it one who practices certain religious ceremonies, goes to church regularly, gives $1/10^{th}$ of his salary regularly? NO is the answer. A Christian is one who has found the Lord Jesus Christ as his or her personal Savior and is related to God. This is not just a verbal confession but both consecration in the heart by trusting in Jesus and confession from the mouth that He is Savior and Lord. This is the Christian who belongs to the Church. He has a relationship with God through the redemptive work on the cross and testifies that Jesus is the Lord and Savior.

The beginning of the book of Philippians introduces us to several people. These people were significant in establishing the church at Philippi. Who are they? What do we learn from them? Will knowing them help us today to do the same thing, that is to establish a local church or be involved in a local church?

The church at Philippi had the involvement of God's people. This involvement led to the establishment of a local church. This accomplishment helps us to know how we, as God's people, can be involved in seeing God's churches established all over the world. There are three different groups of people who played a significant role as a team in the establishment of the church.

1. Paul, with his implicit obedience, plays an important role:

It is Paul the apostle who founded this church at Philippi. The story of this church tells us how it all happened. Notice two components with regards to this accomplishment; namely Paul's vision and Paul's visits.

Firstly, Paul had a vision. Have you ever wondered about what's happening in and with your life? Are you one of those who would say, "Why on earth I am being used? Wide doors are open for me. I am witnessing to people all around. My time here on earth doesn't seem to be wasted but is constantly invested in the lives of others. I am able to visit people in need, talk to people in need and people tell me that I am a 'people-oriented person.'" Well, if you are thinking in that way, here is the answer! You have a radical commitment to Christ and it is the LORD who enables you to have such a wonderful life on this earth. Paul had this life experience because he was radically committed to Him. Do you have that radical commitment? By radical commitment, I mean you are totally committed to Christ every moment of your life and you live 100% for Christ.

The Lord brought a wonderful day in my own life sometime during 1973 when I was 19 years old. It was a day when I had to make a radical decision that would affect the rest of my life. I encountered a major decision in my life. What would I do with my life? Would I become an engineer and earn money and give it to God? Yes, that was my urge inside. It sounded good and noble, but there was no peace in my heart. I decided to take my Bible and go to the nearby lake. There is a famous lake in Hyderabad that was walking distance from my house at the time. I went there alone and knelt down on the rocks crying out to God for peace. There was no peace. Then I turned to the Bible and read some comforting portions. The Word was good but there was still no peace. It was only later that I would realize why I had no peace. I returned home and went into my room, closed the door, knelt down and prayed. This prayer was very different from my "normal" prayers. It was an expression from the heart, utterances of words that were strange to normal desires of my flesh and the prayer was: *Lord I commit to you in total surrender without holding anything. All my future, everything I am and everything I have is yours from this very moment. Take me, use me and I will obey You.* Soon after that prayer something I longed for happened. There was a great peace in my heart that flooded my soul. I got up from my knees and found not only wide-open doors but I also began to see the cost I would pay for rest of my life for following Christ.

Now what about people who don't respond to the call of the Gospel in faith? There are many, many questions that arise for them: "Why on earth am I living?" "How should I spend my time?" "Why do I spend so much time in front of the TV?" "Why am I not being used of the Lord?" The answer is simple! You are not radically committed to Christ. Please listen to what Paul says about his vision in Acts 26:19 "Therefore, O King Agrippa, I was not disobedient to the heavenly vision."

Yes, Paul had a vision and he was willing to go through any kind of persecution in life. While in prison, he wrote the book of Philippians, Colossians, Ephesians and Philemon, known as prison epistles. His time was not wasted even in prison because he had a vision for his life. The word used in Acts 26:19 for vision is: ὀπτασίᾳ This means "to see." Paul saw Jesus in His vision and, when he saw Him, Paul fell to the ground. What happened to John the apostle when he saw Jesus? "When I saw Him, I fell at His feet as though dead. But He laid His right hand on me, saying, 'Fear not, I am the first and the last' " (Rev. 1:17).

How does one apply these truths? Have you seen the Lord with your "spiritual eyes" as you read His Word and meditate on His word? Or are you in hurry to finish your Bible reading? When you hear Him and see Him, do you humble yourself and fall at His feet? In other words, do you fall from your pride, arrogance, stubbornness, hate and all that is of sin and commit yourself to Him?

Secondly, we will look at Paul's visits. His visits are very much connected to his vision. Paul visited Philippi as a result of his vision.

> **Acts 16:9-12** [9] And a vision appeared to Paul in the night: a man of Macedonia was standing there, urging him and saying, "Come over to Macedonia and help us." [10] And when Paul had seen the vision, immediately we sought to go on into Macedonia, concluding that God had called us to preach the Gospel to them. [11] So, setting sail from Troas, we made a direct voyage to Samothrace, and the following day to Neapolis, [12] and from there to Philippi, which is a leading city of the district of Macedonia and a Roman colony. We remained in this city some days.

Philippi was founded by a great Macedonian King by the name of Phillip. The city of Philippi was situated in northeastern Greece and was an island. It appears that Jews were somewhat scarce because there was no synagogue in this city. But Paul's visit to this city did not go to waste. Nothing Paul did was in vain because of his vision. This vision gave him a purpose in life; his life would never be wasted. What does he say, for example, to the Thessalonians? "For you yourselves know, brothers, that our coming to you was not in vain" (1 Thess. 2:1).

God had a purpose in bringing Paul to the city of Philippi. A church had to be planted and established. How would this happen? We will learn more as we look at Lydia.

2. Lydia, with her incredible openness:

Who is this Lydia? Why is Paul associated with this lady? The Bible has the answers. Perhaps you've thought Paul was hostile toward ladies. No, he was not.
Let us look at two key aspects of Lydia's life. Her heart was opened for conversion and her house was opened for a church.

Firstly, we will look at how Lydia and her whole household were converted. Lydia was a businesswoman who sold purple goods.

> **Acts 16:14-15** [14] One who heard us was a woman named Lydia, from the city of Thyatira, a seller of purple goods, who was a worshiper of God. The Lord opened her heart to pay attention to what was said by Paul. [15] And after she was baptized, and her household as well, she urged us, saying, "If you have judged me to be faithful to the Lord, come to my house and stay." And she prevailed upon us.

Lydia's heart was opened by the Lord. She responded to the Word of God and obeyed by being baptized. It is evident that there was no delay in her obedience. What is your response to God's commands today and will you obey today? What a blessing Lydia must have had to be in the city of Philippi and to see a church established in her own house. Your obedience to the Lord with no reservations can lead you to great opportunities in the ministry for the Lord. Somebody said, "If you want plant for a life, plant a tree and if you want to plant for eternity, plant a church." Lydia was an available person in the hands of the Lord. If the Lord is moving and convicting you, are you hardening your heart or are you ready to respond in obedience? Consider

The Lord Uses People to Establish a Local Church

God's warning in Psalm 95:8: "do not harden your hearts, as at Meribah, as on the day at Massah in the wilderness."

Lydia was from a Gentile background. Her conversion was followed by obedience in the waters of baptism. We need such obedience in the church; not just that one person would obey but that whole families would be obedient to God.

Secondly, Lydia's house was available to establish a church. The church at Philippi was founded in 50 A.D. Ladies are not undervalued, especially by Paul. Paul accepted an invitation from this lady. "And after she was baptized, and her household as well, she urged us, saying, 'If you have judged me to be faithful to the Lord, come to my house and stay.' And she prevailed upon us"(Acts 16:15)."So they went out of the prison and visited Lydia. And when they had seen the brothers, they encouraged them and departed"(Acts 16:40).

It is interesting to note the people who are converted; first, Lydia and her household, then a demon-possessed girl and then a jailor and his household.

3. Others with their inspiring offers:

Planting a church is not a job for one man. It is a team effort. How should a team be involved in this ministry? There are two necessary components. These are first, the offering of lives and second, the order of converts.

Firstly, the lives recorded in the story as the church is planted in Philippi are inspiring. Please look at the narration of Luke in:

Acts 16:10-22 ¹⁰ And when Paul had seen the vision, immediately **we** sought to go on into Macedonia, concluding that God had called us to preach the Gospel to them. ¹¹ So, setting sail from Troas, **we** made a direct voyage to Samothrace, and the following day to Neapolis, ¹² and from there to Philippi, which is a leading city of the district of Macedonia and a Roman colony. **We** remained in this city some days. ¹³ And on the Sabbath day **we** went outside the gate to the riverside, where **we** supposed there was a place of prayer, and **we** sat down and spoke to the women who had come together. ¹⁴ One who heard us was a woman named Lydia, from the city of Thyatira, a seller of purple goods, who was a worshiper of God. The Lord opened her heart to pay attention to what was said by Paul. ¹⁵ And after she was baptized, and her household as well, she urged **us**, saying, "If you have judged me to be faithful to the Lord, come to my house and stay." And she prevailed upon **us**. ¹⁶ As **we** were going to the place of prayer, **we** were met by a slave girl who had a spirit of divination and brought her owners much gain by fortune-telling. ¹⁷ She followed Paul and **us**, crying out, "These men are servants of the Most High God, who proclaim to you the way of salvation." ¹⁸ And this she kept doing for many days. Paul, having become greatly annoyed, turned and said to the spirit, "I command you in the name of Jesus Christ to come out of her." And it came out that very hour. ¹⁹ But when her owners saw that their hope of gain was gone, they seized Paul and Silas and dragged them into the marketplace before the rulers. ²⁰ And when they had brought them to the magistrates, they said, "These men are Jews, and they are disturbing our city. ²¹ They advocate customs that are not lawful for us as Romans to accept or practice." [22] The crowd joined in attacking them, and the magistrates tore the garments off them and gave orders to beat them with rods.

The plural pronoun indicates that the writer, Luke, is part of the team with Paul and Silas. They travelled together, witnessed together and faced extreme persecution. Just think of what these men went through for the sake of the Gospel and church planting, how they risked their very lives.

Secondly, the order of those converted is most striking. There was not one particular race in the church but different races and backgrounds were present. According to one scholar, Lightfoot, "The one an Asiatic, the other a Greek, the third a Roman." (Lightfoot, 1898)[1] It is probable that these representatives were part of the first group of believers in the church at Philippi.

So there were Asians, Greeks and Romans. The three had worked in different occupations. Lightfood further says, "In the relations of everyday life they have nothing in common: the first is engaged in an important and lucrative branch of traffic: the second, treated by the law as a mere chattel without any social or political rights, is employed by her masters to trade upon the credulous superstition of the ignorant: the third, equally removed from both the one and the other, holds a subordinate office no less apart." (Lightfoot, 1898)[2] One was in business, another was a soothsayer and the third was a Roman jailor. Their lives were radically changed. The soothsayer specifically left her business and was now a child of God.

---

1. Lightfoot, J.B., Saint Paul's Epistle to the Phillippians, Macmillan And co, New York, 1898, P54.

2. Ibd;

Our church, EastWestCommunityChurch, in Reseda, California, is a good example of the different cultural representations in the church. There are people from Pakistan, Sri Lanka, Fiji, India and the United States. When we get to heaven, we will have people from all nationalities and cultures.

Revelation 7:9-10 [9] After this I looked, and behold, a great multitude that no one could number, from every nation, from **all tribes and peoples and languages**, standing before the throne and before the Lamb, clothed in white robes, with palm branches in their hands, [10] and crying out with a loud voice, "Salvation belongs to our God who sits on the throne, and to the Lamb!"

Conclusion: We cannot say that we don't have "Pauls" to establish churches. It is God who establishes churches but He uses people for that purpose! He uses ordinary people who are totally and radically committed to Him.

We need churches today to be planted all over the world. We have Pakistan, India, Sri Lanka, the USA, Fiji and many nations where churches must be established. Are you involved in this purpose of God?

The life of C.T. Studd provides a wonderful illustration of a man who was totally and radically committed to Jesus Christ. He was a world famous cricketer of his day, probably like, Ian Bothom or Imran Khan, or Kapil Dev or …some famous Sri Lankan Cricketer. C.T.'s story not only enlightens but stirs our hearts. I read his biography during 1978 and was greatly blessed. Norman Grubb, who writes Studd's biography, points out the sacrifices prior to marriage of Studd and his wife-to-be, Priscilla. Studd explained to his would-be-wife that he

The Lord Uses People to Establish a Local Church

gave away all his money to missions and kept only a little bit for their wedding. In reply, Priscilla told CT that if CT didn't give away even that money to missions, Priscilla would not become his wife! What sacrifice! Later in life, CT and Priscilla founded a mission agency called World Wide Evangelical Crusade and there are literally hundreds of missionaries laboring for the Lord around the world as a result of their radical, sacrificial commitment to Christ!

Chapter 2

True Christians Have a Significant Relationship with the Lord

Text: Philippians 1:1-2 Paul and Timothy, servants of Christ Jesus, To all the saints in Christ Jesus who are at Philippi, with the overseers and deacons: ^{2} Grace to you and peace from God our Father and the Lord Jesus Christ.

Introduction: Police aren't perfect, but this cop comes close to winning the ingenuity award! A driver did the right thing, stopping at the school crosswalk, even though he could have beaten the red light by accelerating through the intersection. The tailgating driver behind him went ballistic, pounding on his horn and screaming in frustration as he missed his chance to drive through the intersection.

Still in mid-rant, he heard a tap on his window and looked up into the face of a very serious police officer. The officer ordered him to exit his car with his hands up. He took the driver to the police station where the driver was searched, fingerprinted, photographed and placed in a cell. After a couple of hours, a policeman approached the cell and opened the door. He escorted the man back to the booking desk where the arresting officer was waiting with the man's personal effects.

The police officer said, "I'm awfully sorry for this mistake. You see, as I pulled up behind your car while you were blowing your horn, flipping the guy off in front of you, and cussing a blue streak at him that I noticed the 'What Would Jesus Do' license plate holder, the 'Follow me to Sunday School' bumper sticker, the chrome plated Christian fish emblem on the trunk and the 'My Boss is a Jewish Carpenter' decal on your back window. Naturally, I assumed you had stolen the car..."

Well that kind of hypocritical lifestyle should certainly not be the pattern of the lives of true believers. This guy had stickers on his car about the Lord but did not follow Christ. The man wasn't living a life that others could pattern their lives after. In the book of Philippians we have a pattern that should be found in the true church.

In Philippians 1:1-2, we read of two different groups of people in the church. Each person in these two groups demonstrates a strong, personal relationship with the Lord. Note that:
1. Leaders in the church have a genuine relationship with the Lord Jesus Christ
2. People in the local church have a genuine relationship with the Lord Jesus Christ

Let's look first at the leadership in the Philippian church.

1. Leaders in the church have a genuine relationship with the Lord Jesus Christ

Phil. 1:1 Paul and Timothy, servants of Christ Jesus

We know from the Scriptures that God uses real people, but what kind of people does He use? Paul is an example for us and we can use his life as a pattern for our ministry: "Brothers, join in imitating me, and keep your eyes on those who walk according to the example you have in us" (Phil. 3:17).

Paul is the author of the book of Philippians but he mentions Timothy's name as well. Paul identifies himself as the writer. Paul omits his title of "apostle" though he includes it in his other epistles. We have learned from the narration in Acts 16 that Paul had a vision and as a result of that, he visited Philippi. His visit was not in vain: "holding fast to the word of life, so that in the day of Christ I may be proud that I did not run in vain or labor in vain"(Phil. 2:16).

God took care the founding of the Philippian church by opening the heart of Lydia. We read in Acts 16:14:"The Lord opened her heart to pay attention to what was said by Paul."

What could have motivated Paul to obey as he did, in following the vision the Lord gave him? His genuine conversion, commitment and consecration! These are essentials for our spiritual life to motivate us each day as well. Do you have them? Look at his conversion in Acts 9, 22, and 26. Think of his commitment when he says in Philippians 1:21-22:"For to me to live is Christ, and to die is gain. If I am to live in the flesh, that means fruitful labor for me. Yet which I shall choose I cannot tell."

His genuine conversion led him to a genuine commitment to Christ and consecration. This made him a genuine, passionate servant of Christ. Listen to Paul's passion in:

> **1 Thessalonians 2:1-2** For you yourselves know, brothers,[1] that our coming to you was not in vain. [2] But though we had already suffered and been shamefully

treated at Philippi, as you know, we had boldness in our God to declare to you the Gospel of God in the midst of much conflict.

Yes, even in much conflict, Paul's commitment to Christ is not in question but is consistent. Do you move about in life because God has told you to do so? Please listen to another motivating factor in his life: "holding fast to the word of life, so that in the day of Christ I may be proud that I did not run in vain or labor in vain" (Phil. 2:16).

Paul's eschatology (doctrine of the end times) was correct. It motivated him to live so as to make his life count for Christ. Paul knew that God will reward some in that day. You, too, are going to face the day of Christ. Are you ready?

Paul then says that he and Timothy are "servants" of Christ Jesus. Paul probably used the term "servants" from an Old Testament concept – the word literally means "slaves." The beginning verses of Joshua speak of Moses being God's servant. Judges 2:8 says that Joshua is the servant of God and David was called as the servant of God in Psalms 78:70; 89:3, 20. Paul not only called himself a slave (or servant) of Christ but he lived that way. This is the pattern for our leaders today. There is a relationship between him and Christ Jesus. Now observing the name "Jesus Christ," we understand that Christ is the title and Jesus is the name. He uses these words many times and in different ways throughout the book of Philippians.

2. People in the church have a genuine relationship with the Lord Jesus Christ

Phil. 1:2 To all the saints in Christ Jesus who are at Philippi, with the overseers and deacons

Let us look at two components of that relationship:

    i) All the saints

Who are these people in the church? In the previous chapter, we saw that the church was composed of many races, cultures and nationalities. We see here that the church at Philippi included Lydia, an Asian, demon-possessed girl, a Greek and Roman jailor! Oh what a mixture of races. Now, these people at Philippi were not just "saved" but saved <u>and became part of the church</u>. Paul calls them "saints." When the Gospel is internalized, one becomes a saint. You are now a "saved sinner" and you are a saint because of the blood of Christ Jesus.

Paul addresses all believers as saints. Please look at:

Ephesians 1:1 To the saints who are in Ephesus, and are faithful in Christ Jesus…

2 Corinthians 1:1 with all the saints who are in the whole of Achaia…

1 Corinthians 1:2 to those sanctified in Christ Jesus, called to be saints together with all those who in every place call upon the name of our Lord Jesus Christ, both their Lord and ours.

    ii) In Christ Jesus

Now, the saints have a relationship with the Lord and that is what Paul addresses. The mention of the Lord's name is very noticeable. Montgomery observes this fact and says "Christ" or "Jesus Christ" occurs 17 times in the first chapter of Philippians alone. It is essential to know these truths in our

Christian life. Every believer is "in Christ." When you know this truth, you will have a radical change in your life. It will affect your walk, your talk, your thoughts, your sight and every aspect of your life. It should affect your married life and your life at your job. You are either in Christ Jesus or you are not! There is no middle ground. If you are in Him, it is because of His grace and not your efforts or your righteousness. We will learn more about grace in the next chapter.

What is the pattern of the local church? The church at Philippi sets the example for us. They established a good structure in the church. They had overseers and deacons, which we will look at more in the next chapter as well.

Conclusion: There is a challenge for those who are in leadership. They are to live as slaves of Christ Jesus alone. They are servants of no one but the Lord of Lords and King of Kings. They are bound to do His will, nothing less and nothing else. People in the church are saints and are in Christ Jesus. They are saints whether they are at church or not. They are to live for God no matter where they are.

Let me illustrate this with a story. Susan Leinen told my wife, Flory, and me about an Indian doctor who is a pediatrician at Northridge Hospital. This lady saw our Shepherding the Nations calendar in the room of Susan's husband, Randy, who was a patient at the hospital. The doctor noticed the word "missions" and "God's work in India." She was drawn to it and her interest led her to visit Randy in the cardiac care unit. When this doctor visited Randy and Susan, she led a powerful time of prayer for Randy and ministered to the hearts of both Randy and Susan. This doctor was a witness. Wherever you are, you can impact the lives of people and live as a powerful witness for Christ.

Chapter 3

God is the Source

Text: ***Philippians 1:2-3*** *[2] **Grace to you and peace from God our Father and the Lord Jesus Christ.** [3] **I thank my God in all my remembrance of you***

Introduction: While everything else is uncertain, only God is "certain!" Everything else may fail, but God will never fail. The Bible gives us a lot of support for this truth. Think of David, the famous king of Israel. Don't you think that he went through struggles in life? For example, look at his words in Psalm 4:1 "Answer me when I call, O God of my righteousness! You have given me relief when I was in distress. Be gracious to me and hear my prayer!" The Hebrew word, הִרְחַבְ means widened or enlarged or relief. David went through lot of difficulties in life. Consider the following passage.

1 Samuel 30:1-8 Now when David and his men came to Ziklag on the third day, the Amalekites had made a raid against the Negeb and against Ziklag. They had overcome Ziklag and burned it with fire [2] and taken captive the women and all[1] who were in it, both small and great. They killed no one, but carried them off and went their way. [3] And when David and his men came to the city, they found it burned with fire, and their wives and sons and daughters taken captive. [4] Then David and the people who were with him raised their voices and wept until they had no more strength to weep. [5] David's two wives also had been taken captive, Ahinoam of Jezreel and Abigail the widow of Nabal of Carmel. [6] And David was greatly distressed, for the people spoke of stoning him, because all the people were bitter in soul,[1] each for his sons and daughters. But David strengthened himself in the LORD his God. [7] And David said to Abiathar the priest, the son of Ahimelech, "Bring me the ephod." So Abiathar brought the ephod to David. [8] And David inquired of the LORD, "Shall I pursue after this band? Shall I overtake them?" He answered him, "Pursue, for you shall surely overtake and shall surely rescue."

Now, what happened as a result of David's inquiring and then pursuing after his enemies? "David recovered all that the Amalekites had taken, and David rescued his two wives. Nothing was missing, whether small or great, sons or daughters, spoil or anything that had been taken. David brought back all" (1 Sam. 30:18-19). Nothing was missing. David recovered all that was lost. Amazing, isn't it? David certainly knew Who was the source of all that he had. It was not his strength or his arm of flesh, but it was God. He went to God and that was his secret.

The Christian experience is positive and powerful. Paul says in Philippians 4:13: "I can do all things through him who strengthens me." Then he encourages the Philippians by saying: "And my God will supply every need of yours according to his riches in glory in Christ Jesus" (Phil. 4:19).

Paul knew the same secret King David knew. Paul writes to the Philippians about grace and peace that comes from God and thanks God for the very remembrance of the church. He thanks God because God is the One who brought these Philippians to him.

God is the source for all spiritual realities and the source in the church for spiritual resources as well.

Here are three acknowledgments Paul makes about the fact that God is the source:

1. God is the source of grace
2. God is the source of peace
3. God is the One who brings the saints together

Firstly, God is the source of grace. When we think of grace, that famous song, *Amazing Grace,* comes to mind. Consider John Newton, the author of the wonderful hymn *Amazing Grace.* John Newton was raised in a Christian home in England in his very early years. But he was orphaned at the age of six and lived with a non-Christian relative. There, Christianity was mocked and he was persecuted. At last, to escape the conditions at home, Newton ran away to sea and became an apprentice seaman in the British Navy. He served in the Navy for some time. Ultimately, he deserted and ran away to Africa. He tells in his own words that he went there for just one purpose: "to sin his fill."

In Africa Newton joined forces with a Portuguese slave trader and was treated very cruelly. At times, the slave trader went away on expeditions and the young man was left in charge of the slave trader's African wife, the head of his harem. She hated all white men and took out her hatred on Newton. He tells that she exercised such power in her husband's absence that he was compelled to eat his food off the dusty floor like a dog.

At last the young Newton fled from this treatment and made his way to the coast where he lit a signal fire and was picked up by a slave ship on its way to England. The captain was

God is the Source

disappointed that Newton had no ivory to sell, but because the young man knew something about navigation, he was made a ship's mate. Newton could not keep even this position. During the voyage he broke into the ship's supply of rum and distributed it to the crew so that the crew became drunk. In a stupor, Newton fell into the sea and was rescued from drowning by one of the officers who speared him with a harpoon, leaving a fist-sized scar in his thigh.

Near Scotland, toward the end of the voyage, Newton's ship encountered heavy winds. It was blown off course and began to sink. Newton was sent down into the hold with the slaves and told to man the pumps. He was frightened to death. He was sure that the ship would sink and that he would drown. He worked at the pumps for days and, as he worked, he began to cry out to God from the hold of the ship. He began to remember verses he had been taught as a child. And as he remembered them, he was miraculously transformed. He was born again. And he went on to become a great preacher and a teacher of the Word of God in England. It was this John Newton who wrote:

> *Amazing grace! How sweet the sound,*
> *That saved a wretch like me!*
> *I once was lost, but now am found;*
> *Was blind, but now I see.* (Boice, 1971)[1]

The word for grace in Greek is *charis*; it is used 155 times in the New Testament and approximately 100 times by Paul in his epistles. Paul uses the word to stress the "unmerited favor" of God. Now this "unmerited favor of God" belongs to believers by faith in Christ and is the source of this grace is God.

---

1. Boice, James Montgomery, Phillippians An expostional Commentary, Zondervan Publishing House, Grand Rapids, Michigan, 1971, p 28,9.

Early on in my Christian experience I tended heavily towards legalism. I believed in "my personal opinions" of what true spiritual life was or should be. For example, consider the posture of our physical bodies when we pray. I thought God would be pleased and hear me ONLY when I prayed on my knees. I remember working one winter in the northwestern part of India in a state called Rajasthan and it was freezing cold! There was an area upstairs which didn't have a roof. I was leading a Gospel team of several people. As was my routine during those years, I would pray prior to falling asleep and unless I did this, I feared that I was displeasing God and that I was going against His will. So I decided to go upstairs under the open sky to kneel down on the floor; this wasn't at all easy for my knees. My legalistic view made me determined to stay therein that shivering cold for forty minutes or so. What was the result? Spirituality? No, I was ill the next day with a high temperature!

Legalism and grace go in opposite directions. While grace allows you to enjoy God's favor and to lead a life of liberty and freedom, legalism brings you under heavy pressure to live in your own strength to earn God's favor. But God's grace is given freely to those who trust in Jesus Christ by faith!

Remember the grace of God:

- Our redemption is based on the grace of God.
  Ephesians 1:7 In him we have redemption through his blood, the forgiveness of our trespasses, according to the riches of his grace.

- Our position is based on the grace of God.
  1 Corinthians 15:10 But by the grace of God I am what I am, and his grace toward me was not in vain. On the

contrary, I worked harder than any of them, though it was not I, but the grace of God that is with me.
- Our <u>glorification</u> is based on God's grace.
1 Peter 5:10 And after you have suffered a little while, the God of all grace, who has called you to his eternal glory in Christ, will himself restore,   confirm, strengthen, and establish you.

Secondly, God is not only the source of grace, but the source of peace and it is freely given. *Eierein*is the Greek word for peace. Paul uses "grace and peace" in his epistles frequently (Rom. 1:7; 1 Cor. 1:3; 2 Cor. 1:2; Gal. 1:3; Eph. 1:2; Phil. 1:2; Col. 1:2; 1 Thess. 1:1;2 Thess. 1:2; Pilm. 3). One commentator, Martin Hawthorne, points out that while "peace" is the standard Jewish greeting, Paul also uses, "grace, mercy and peace" in 1 Timothy 1:2 and Titus 1:2. Paul combines both Western and Eastern types of greetings. Paul's mention of peace doesn't just refer to "well-being" but to harmony, tranquility, wholeness, salvation, and reconciliation. (Lightfoot, 1898)[2] This is the activity of God in a believer's life. This activity begins the moment a sinner repents from sin and turns to God.

Consider this peace:

- It is peace that comes from God.
  Numbers 6:26 the LORD lift up his countenance upon you and give you peace.

- It is peace with God.
  Romans 5:1 Therefore, since we have been justified by faith, we have peace with God through our Lord Jesus Christ.

---

2. Hawthorne, Gerald F.: Word Biblical Commentary, Nelson Reference & Electronic, 2004, P 12

- It is peace with others.
  Hebrews 12:14 Strive for peace with everyone, and for the holiness without which no one will see the Lord.

This peace comes from God the Father and the Lord Jesus Christ. Paul has a proper understanding of the doctrine of God and Christology. He puts these two persons of the Godhead on an equal level.

"Father" speaks of an intimate relationship with God. This relationship is established by the process given in John 1:12:"But as many as received Him, to them He gave the right to become children of God, even to those who believe in His name."

Every child of God has the privilege of calling God, "Father." Can anything bad come from the Father's hand? Whatever comes from His hand is most precious and best! Paul knew his theology well. That is why he could put God and the Lord Jesus Christ on the same, equal level. Have you heard the song lyrics, "Abba, Father, let me be yours and yours alone"? When you come into the grips of this intimacy, you want to be HIS and HIS alone.

Thirdly, Paul says, "I thank my God." The Philippians encouraged Paul by their contributions and these became their reason to thank God, but why is Paul not thanking the Philippians at the very outset? Because instead he is thanking God! He thanks God because it is God who brought the Philippian believers to him and so whenever Paul remembers the Philippians, he thanks God.

These believers became very special to Paul because:

- They cared for him.
  Philippians 4:15-16 [15] And you Philippians yourselves know that in the beginning of the Gospel, when I left Macedonia, no church entered into partnership with me in giving and receiving, except you only. [16] Even in Thessalonica you sent me help for my needs once and again.

- They had a man like Timothy who was concerned for them.
  Philippians 2:19-20 [19] I hope in the Lord Jesus to send Timothy to you soon, so that I too may be cheered by news of you. [20] For I have no one like him, who will be genuinely concerned for your welfare.

God is the one who brought the saints at Philippi together. The Philippians were therefore Paul's reason for thanksgiving. Paul is not forgetful of their deeds or actions or participation in the Gospel. It is God who opened the heart of Lydia. It is God who healed the demon possessed girl and it is God who mightily worked in the prison when the jailor got saved and his household was baptized. How can this attitude of Paul be yours today? How can <u>you</u> be thankful now? The Word of God exhorts, commands and motivates us to thank God. Please look at these verses:

Psalm 100:4 Enter his gates with thanksgiving, and his courts with praise! Give thanks to him; bless his name!

Romans 1:21 For although they knew God, they did not honor him as God or give thanks to him, but they became futile in their thinking, and their foolish hearts were darkened.

Colossians 3:15 And let the peace of Christ rule in your hearts, to which indeed you were called in one body. And be thankful.

Psalm 35:18 I will thank you in the great congregation; in the mighty throng I will praise you.

Psalm 92:1 It is good to give thanks to the LORD, to sing praises to your name, O Most High...

Psalm 136:1-3 Give thanks to the LORD, for he is good, for his steadfast love endures forever. [2] Give thanks to the God of gods, for his steadfast love endures forever. [3] Give thanks to the Lord of lords, for his steadfast love endures forever...

God wants us to have thankful hearts! Remember Shakespeare's statement: "How sharper than a serpent's tooth it is to have a thankless child." Jesus illustrates this picture of a heart of gratitude and an unthankful heart in the following passage:

> **Luke 17:12-18** [2] And as he entered a village, he was met by ten lepers, who stood at a distance [13] and lifted up their voices, saying, "Jesus, Master, have mercy on us." [14] When he saw them he said to them, "Go and show yourselves to the priests." And as they went they were cleansed. [15] Then one of them, when he saw that he was healed, turned back, praising God with a loud voice; [16] and he fell on his face at Jesus' feet, giving him thanks. Now he was a Samaritan. [17] Then Jesus answered, "Were not ten cleansed? Where are the nine? [18] Was no one found to return and give praise to God except this foreigner?"

God is the Source

Do you want to enjoy the grace of God? It is free for you at every moment of your life. Do you want to enjoy the peace of God? This is yours freely from God and with God if you have surrendered your life to Christ. But are you striving to keep peace with each other? Is there a need for you to reconcile with someone? Go to God and pray for forgiveness. Then, go to that person with whom you don't have peace and ask for his or her forgiveness. This is revival. This is honoring to God. When the Lord returns, you will not be ashamed.

Chapter 4

Integral Connections within believers

Text: *Philippians 1:4-6* [4] *always offering prayer with joy in my every prayer for you all,* [5] *in view of your participation in the Gospel from the first day until now.* [6]*For I am confident of this very thing, that He who began a good work in you will perfect it until the day of Christ Jesus.*

Introduction: What connects you to each other? For some it is location, for others it is religion. For some it is status and for others it is spirituality. It is interesting to see the networking, internet, and worldwide web in operation. Then there are Facebook and Skype. All of these are connecting people with each other. Do you know that there is an even more wonderful connection between believers? It is more powerful, dynamic, and exciting than all these electronic media as we shall see.

One of the most enjoyable times I ever had in life was serving on the Logos ship for a little over five months. For those who do not know what this Logos ship is, let me briefly explain. A group of young people in the U.S. started praying for six years for a ship that would serve as a vessel to take people around the world to preach the Gospel. And the Lord gave them a ship which they named "Logos."

Those who sailed on this ship were all believers, committed to the Lord and to world evangelism. This group

Integral Connections within believers

included the captain, officers and engineers. When I was on this ship during 1974, there were people from 22 nations! These people came from different nations, languages, cultures and backgrounds. There was a common pantry and a common dining hall. There were strict guidelines for our conduct such as weekly prayers from 8 p.m. till 2 a.m. and devotions every day for all the people aboard the ship. It was a wonderful, living testimony of harmonious relationships. What was the secret to this unity? There was a strong emphasis on prayer. There was also an explicit partnership in the Gospel and God's good work was evident in the life of each believer.

Here are the three integral connections for unity and integrity based on Philippians 1:4-6:

1. The connection that comes through prayer
2. The connection that comes through partnership
3. The connection that comes through the permanent work of God

Connections emerge through prayer, connections that are intertwined through partnership and connections that are established through the permanent work of God. These produce unity and integrity. These are not superficial cords, not strings that connect because of color, culture or country but spiritual connections that knit man and God forever and believers with one another.

1. The connection that comes through prayer

Phil. 1:4 always offering prayer with joy in my every prayer for you all

While I was growing up in Hyderabad as a young Christian, I had a friend who took me to a ladies prayer meeting. The ladies gathered for regular fasting once a week or so. As a teenager, these ladies were like mothers and aunties and allowed us to participate with them in prayer. The host of this group was a prayerful lady who was very fond of us. Later, when I had to leave Hyderabad to work in North India, it was this sister who hosted the prayer time at her house who kept in contact with me. In one of her letters to me, she said these words, "Ryder, I meet with you regularly at the feet of the Lord Jesus Christ." What a way to stay connected - at the very feet of the Lord in PRAYER!

Prayer is a wonderful means to keep connections with each other. Paul says he "always" prays! There were two key characteristics of Paul's prayer; it was constant and it was cheerful.

Firstly, it is a continuous prayer. Paul not only commands others to pray continuously but he does so himself. Please look at what he says in 1 Thessalonians 5:17. We are to "pray without ceasing." Let me illustrate this further with our Lord's teaching on the same topic in:

> **Luke 18:1-7** Now He was telling them a parable to show that at all times they ought to pray and not to lose heart, [2] saying, "In a certain city there was a judge who did not fear God and did not respect man. [3] "There was a widow in that city, and she kept coming to him, saying, 'Give me legal protection from my opponent.' [4] "For a while he was unwilling; but afterward he said to himself, 'Even though I do not fear God nor respect man, [5] yet because this widow bothers me, I will give her legal protection, otherwise by continually coming she will wear me out.'" [6] And the Lord said, "Hear what

Integral Connections within believers

the unrighteous judge said; ⁷ now, will not God bring about justice for His elect who cry to Him day and night, and will He delay long over them?

Writing about Paul's kind of prayer, Dwight Pentecost in his book on Philippians says, "The Apostle Paul has a phenomenal prayer life. He has either a remarkable memory or an unusually long prayer list, for ten years after his initial contact with the city of Philippi he is able still to remember the Philippians by name, and he prays for them repeatedly." (Pentecost, 1973)[1] Do you have a prayer list? Do you feel the need to pray for others? The Bible teaches us to pray for others. Here in the text, we have an exhortation to pray constantly. This speaks of constant dependency on God, a consistent walk with God, a complimenting spiritual life and a conspicuous connection with others for whom you pray.

Dwight Pentecost says that Paul prays for the Philippians individually and continually. When I looked at this fact, I was compelled in my heart to put aside what I was doing at that time and set my heart right with God. I remembered the years past when I had a long list of prayer requests, remembering people all over the world but I had lost this. I needed to confess my sin before God. I pleaded with God to restore me to this prayer life. Today, it is my plea with you: Do you have your healthy prayer life?

Another scholar, R.C.H. Lenski, describes the grammar in Philippians 1:3 and says that "always" and "every" flow

---

1. Pentecost, J. Dwight: The Joy of Living A Study of Phillippians, The Zondervan Corporation, Grand Rapids, Mich, 1973, p 15.

together.[2] He further observes that it denotes "continuous, ever-repeated petition." [3]Lenski observes that "all" includes "all children," "all backward and faulty members" [4] and hence Paul has a longsuffering, patient heart in order to pray in this fashion. Paul didn't get tired of prayer.

Secondly, Paul's prayer is a cheerful prayer. Paul says he prays with joy. This word group "joy and rejoice" occur 16 times in this book of Philippians. If you remember, Paul is writing this epistle from a prison. Paul petitions with joy in his heart. The very remembrance of the Philippians brings him joy. Even though he is imprisoned, his heart and mind were set on God who is good. He trusts and believes good will happen in spite of this bad experience. Paul writes: "And most of the brothers, having become confident in the Lord by my imprisonment, are much more bold to speak the word without fear" (Phil. 1:14).

Because of his adequate knowledge of theology and his admirable understanding of God, he is able to exhort others to set their hearts and minds not on what they were going through but on God. Paul states: "Finally, brothers, whatever is true, whatever is honorable, whatever is just, whatever is pure, whatever is lovely, whatever is commendable, if there is any excellence, if there is anything worthy of praise, think about these things" (Phil. 4:8).

---

2. Lenski, R.C.H., The Interpretation of St. Paul's Epistles to the Galations to the Ephesians and to the Philippians, Augsburg Publishing House, Minneapolis, Minnesota, 1961, p 706

3. Ibid p 707

4. Ibid p 707

Integral Connections within believers

In the most difficult times of life, Paul knew how to rejoice and pray and he prayed with joy. How do you pray? Paul's prayer caused a wonderfully strong connection with the Philippian people.

2. The connection that comes through partnership

Phil. 1:5 because of your partnership in the Gospel from the first day until now.

Please note that verse 4 has a connection to verse 5 and therefore the comma that comes after verse 4 in our versions should be disregarded. The word Gospel occurs more in this book than in any of Paul's other epistles. The word *koinonia*, translated as "fellowship" in the King James Version refers to "participating" in something rather than sharing something. In Urdu, it is translated like this: "is liye ki tum awwal roz se lekar aj tak khushkhabari ke phailane men sharik rahe ho;" In Hindi it is translated as: "kyonki pahele hi din se aaj thak thum susamachar mein mere sahabhagi rahe ho." In the English Standard Version, it is translated well when we read "partnership."

Partnership here has a broad meaning. One scholar, Lenski, says "your fellowship as regards the Gospel is as broad as Acts 2:42, the fellowship of faith in the Gospel, of confession of the Gospel, of worship and of Christian life in the grace of the Gospel." This partnership is much broader than simply the sharing of money. The Philippians sent monetary gifts to Paul three times. But their partnership in the Gospel is significantly more meaningful to Paul and expressed the love of the Philippians even more than their monetary gift. The Gospel has reconciled us to God and to each other. The power of the Gospel does a mighty work in the lives of people. "For I am not ashamed of the Gospel, for it is the power of God for salvation to everyone who believes, to the Jew first and also to the Greek" (Rom. 1:16).

Let me illustrate. When you are reconciled with God and with man, your reconciliation is expressed outwardly. There is a great illustration of this in:

> **Luke 19:8-10** [8] And Zacchaeus stood and said to the Lord, "Behold, Lord, the half of my goods I give to the poor. And if I have defrauded anyone of anything, I restore it fourfold." [9] And Jesus said to him, "Today salvation has come to this house, since he also is a son of Abraham. [10] For the Son of Man came to seek and to save the lost."

Zaccheus did exactly as the Lord had instructed him. His salvation had an outward manifestation. The Philippians had a partnership with the Gospel; it was not merely a partnership with Paul but also with each other.

The Gospel is a constant reminder to us of our reconciliation with God, with ourselves and with each other. Is this a reality in your life? Do you have partnership with the Gospel? Between the events that occurred in Acts 16 and the time of Paul's writing, ten years have passed. Their partnership in the Gospel was evident throughout these many years.

3. The connection that comes through permanent work of God

Phil. 1:6 And I am sure of this, that he who began a good work in you will bring it to completion at the day of Jesus Christ.

Integral Connections within believers

Let us observe three components of God's Work:

i) The commencement of God's work
ii) The confidence in God's work
iii) The completion of God's work

Firstly, Paul acknowledges that it is God who began His good work. It was not Paul's work but God's, though Paul labored hard at Philippi. God's work within a believer begins the moment we are converted or respond to His call. Paul said, "But by the grace of God I am what I am, and his grace toward me was not in vain. On the contrary, I worked harder than any of them, though it was not I, but the grace of God that is with me" (1 Cor. 15:10).

Secondly, Paul describes God's work with the adjective "good." He says it is a "good" work. Your salvation is God's good work in your life. Let people mock you or say anything to you but salvation is God's good work in you. The Greek word for "good" is **avgaqo.** It means "good; useful, satisfactory for one's (its) purpose, fitting, beneficial, sound (of trees), fertile (of soil), happy (of days), in a moral sense upright, just, kind, generous, clear (of conscience), perfect, inherently good (of God), to. avgaqo,n the good, what is good, what is right or upright, what is beneficial or advantageous, ta. avgaqa, goods, possessions, good things (Luke 16:25) and good deeds (John 5:29)."

Thirdly, Paul tells us the duration and time of completion of God's work. Please listen to this. When will God complete His good work in your life? Paul answers "at the day of Jesus Christ." This refers to the last day of the world. That is the day when the Lord appears and the souls of His saints who have died are united with their bodies and believers who are still alive

Integral Connections within believers

are caught up to be with Him. Yes, until the end, He will carry on His good work in your life. He will not give up on you. You may be confident of this as Paul was confident. The word for confidence, pei, qw, means to have confidence, be confident, be certain or be sure. You have a God who not only begins and does a good work but also completes it at His day.

Conclusion: We are living in an historic time. The world is different than it was years ago. In August 2003 it was estimated that 160 to 162 million Americans were "online." That means there were millions who had some means for getting connected with each other. There is a new Bible product that is made by Tyndale Publishers. It is called Ilumina which has 10,000 Bible notes, maps, drawings, etc. This complex computer program connects one to so much knowledge. Yes, we are living in a world that has advanced so much but don't you want to experience the beautiful life and relationships that God describes in Philippians? This is available to those who know Him, are connected through prayer, through their partnership in the Gospel and through their participation in the Gospel. These saints have a confidence that, without a doubt, God began a good work in them and He will complete it at His day!

Chapter 5

Bound by Inseparable Ties

Text: *Philippians 1:7-9* ⁷ *It is right for me to feel this way about you all, because I hold you in my heart, for you are all partakers with me of grace, both in my imprisonment and in the defense and confirmation of the Gospel.* ⁸ *For God is my witness, how I yearn for you all with the affection of Christ Jesus.* ⁹ *And it is my prayer that your love may abound more and more, with knowledge and all discernment*

Introduction: Are there any ties that bind people together? People can easily lose the connection with others. I have watched politics in different countries and Indian politics seem to excel in politicians changing their political ties according to their whims. There are not very many who will be found loyal to one party and be tied to that party. The same thing is true with Christian organizations. During our mission trips to India we have heard how people like to jump from one organization to another depending on where there is more money. People are also fickle in marriages, moving from one partner to another. What is wrong in all these situations? The problem is that people do not have strong ties with each other. The strings and chords that should bind are weak.

Think of the bonds in Christian relationships - be it with each other or with God. They are strong because they are from God. They are divine. Paul's relationship and connections with those in the church in Philippi reflect an extremely strong bond.

What leads to strong ties?

Here are some characteristics of these inseparable ties:

1. These ties are based on internal relationships: v. 7
2. These ties are manifested by a genuine longing: v. 8
3. These ties are manifested by prayer: v. 9

It is said about the book of Philippians that it is a very affectionate epistle of Paul. There is appreciation and affection expressed between Paul and the church. There was a close and good connection between the two and this is a good example for all of us. While I was studying this passage, I received a phone call from the Ghosh family. Robin Ghosh greeted me with, "Happy Resurrection Day!" and then invited me over to eat puri and halwa. This demonstrated affection and intimacy to me. There is a very strong link and connection between believers.

1. These ties are based on internal relationship: v. 7

Phil. 1:7 It is right for me to feel this way about you all, because I hold you in my heart, for you are all partakers with me of grace, both in my imprisonment and in the defense and confirmation of the Gospel

Two key characteristics of this internal relationship are a right feeling from the heart and grace, which is the reason for the tie. According to scholar, Lenski, the translation "it is right for me" is correct. Paul has a right feeling about the church at Philippi. This is an internal relationship. Paul says he holds the Philippians in his heart so then it is not an external tie because it is in the heart.

What is the reason for these strong ties between believers? It is grace. The reason for Paul's affection for these believers is not human but divine – they are all partakers of grace. There is no difference in the "grace" of one versus another. It is the same for Paul as for the believers at Philippi. The moment we are saved, we are partakers of God's grace. Paul says, "For by grace you have been saved through faith. And this is not your own doing; it is the gift of God, not a result of works, so that no one may boast" (Eph. 2:8-9).

2. These ties are based on genuine longing: v. 8

Phil. 1:8 For God is my witness, how I yearn for you all with the affection of Christ Jesus.

Note two components of Paul's longing:

i) God alone is the witness of Paul's life. Paul is not afraid to say this because his heart is pure, his intentions are genuine and when God judges, Paul is confident that he will not be found guilty.
ii) Paul's affection is not human but from Christ Jesus. He draws affection from the Lord.

3. These ties are based on prayer: v. 9

Phil. 1:9 And it is my prayer that your love may abound more and more, with knowledge and all discernment.

There are two parts to Paul's prayer. First, consider Paul's plea. The God of love who hears prayers and answers them can take care of Paul's request. Paul prays for an important aspect that affects all relationships; love. Love covers sin and binds us to one another. "Hatred stirs up strife, but love covers all offenses" (Prov. 10:12). "But the fruit of the Spirit is love, joy, peace, patience, kindness, goodness, faithfulness, gentleness, self-control; against such things there is no law" (Gal. 5:22-23).

Second, consider Paul's plea for love with knowledge and discernment. Our love should be based in knowledge (understanding in the heart) and insight, not just superficial love that leads nowhere.

Let me conclude with a question, do you see a need in your life for a very strong link and connection between believers. Think of the bonds in Christian relationships - be it with each other or with God. They are strong because they are from God. Be bound by the eternal ties.

Chapter 6

Preparing for the Day of Christ

Text: *Philippians 1:9-11* *[9]And it is my prayer that your love may abound more and more, with knowledge and all discernment[10]so that you may approve what is excellent, and so be pure and blameless for the day of Christ, [11] filled with the fruit of righteousness that comes through Jesus Christ, to the glory and praise of God.*

Introduction: Preparation is a key facet of every person's life. Consider the many ways we prepare for various aspects of life:

- Some may prepare to get up in the morning
- Some may prepare to have a quiet time with the Lord in the morning
- Some may prepare for how they will dress for work
- Some may prepare for the events of the day
- Some may be preparing for marriage
- Some may be preparing for a new job
- Some may be preparing for a party
- Some may be preparing for a vacation
- Some may be preparing for church service

And beyond all these preparations, everyone should be preparing for the Day of Christ. Are you? The Bible says, there is going to be a great day! I am speaking about the Day of the

Christ. Now the Lord's Day and the Day of the Lord are not the same. The Apostle John talks about the Lord's Day in Revelation 1:10. This happened during the time he was on the island called Patmos as a consequence of preaching the Gospel. This is the only place in the NT where we find this expression. In other places this day is referred to as the first day of the week, which is Sunday. It was on Sunday that the early church began to meet for worship services as recorded in Acts 20:7 and 1 Corinthians 16:2. In Philippians, though, Paul is talking about the other day which is called The Day of the Lord. This is the day the Lord will appear in His second advent. How are we to prepare for that day? I am not talking about how well dressed you will be or how decorated you will be or what kind of cologne you'll put on but those garments you'll wear to meet our Lord in the air. Imagine, the Lord is coming and He can come at any moment. The moment He appears, the church will be caught up to meet Him and will be presented to Him. Are you ready and are you prepared?

So how should we prepare for the Day of Christ? We need to be focused and we need to be filled.

1. Be focused.

Phil. 1:10 so that you may approve what is excellent, and so be pure and blameless for the day of Christ

On what should we focus? What are the qualities that will make you "presentable" when the Lord appears? There is a clear focus that is found in what Paul is saying to the Philippians. He is using himself as the model for preparation. He points out the qualities that need to be found in believers in order to prepare for the day of Christ.

Preparing for the Day of Christ

Paul's prayer was focused. Please note the words "so that" in Philippians 1:10. This draws your attention to the previous verse. Have you ever done any bird watching or watched those who do bird watch? Bird watchers are suddenly attracted to either a single bird or many birds. They describe, point out, and make sounds while watching birds.

How about watching God's people? How do they pray? How do they have their quiet time? How do they preach? How do they counsel? You can make observations in person or by reading or hearing about other exemplary Christians. We can learn many lessons from them. Please remember what Paul prayed for in Phil. 1:9 for the Philippians. "And it is my prayer that your love may abound more and more, with knowledge and all discernment" (Phil. 1:9).

Paul prayed for love with "knowledge and discernment." This "agape" love would "overflow" or "excel" or "abound" in believers who have "knowledge" and "insight" or "judgment" or "discernment." Bible scholar Lenski observes this as "stronger, wiser, abler love." Love is no ordinary attribute. It flows out, expresses and demonstrates itself. How important it is to have this kind of love, love that is "abler." There is a reason for Paul's focus and it is mentioned in verse 10, "so that one may approve what is excellent, and so be pure and blameless."

Paul focused on specific qualities; what is *excellent* in order to be *pure* and *blameless*. He wants to prove what is excellent, then purity and blamelessness follow. The word used for "approve" is: δοκιμάζω (dokimazo) which means "test, examine; interpret, discern, discover; approve; prove, demonstrate."[1]. This word refers to the testing of metals and

---

1. Bible Works, 6.0

coins in order to see any mixture of alloy. In New Testament times, the coins were sometimes mixed with impurities and were "too base alloy." Testing would reveal the differences and the imperfections.

So approve what is "excellent." διαφέρω (aor. subj. διενέγκω) means to be superior to, τὰ δ. what is best or right (Rom. 2:18, Phil. 1:10), differ, differ from, carry through (Mark 11:16). How would you do this? The answer is "by testing." Test your talk, your thinking, the things you do, your relationships, your ministry and everything in your life. We need to do this to be pure (εἰλικρινής, ές pure, sincere, honest) and blameless (ἀπρόσκοπος, ον blameless, faultless, inoffensive, clear conscience). If you want to be pure and blameless, you need to confess what you are. If you want to know what you are, you need to look at yourself. This happens by self examination. "Search me, O God, and know my heart! Try me and know my thoughts! And see if there be any grievous way in me, and lead me in the way everlasting!" (Ps. 139:23-24).

A genuine believer should search his or her heart all the time. The moment you sin in thought or deed you must be willing to confess it and get rid of it. This happens by personally going to the Lord each time you sin and asking His forgiveness. At the same time, if you have sinned against somebody, you should go and confess it to that particular person and ask forgiveness clearly, fearlessly and with humility.

Consider this example. When King David sinned, he was honest in confessing to God. Please look at his story and refresh your mind by observing what has happened in the history of Israel. David was a great king but he failed and sinned.

Preparing for the Day of Christ

1 Chronicles 21:1-17 Then Satan stood against Israel and incited David to number Israel. ² So David said to Joab and the commanders of the army, "Go, number Israel, from Beersheba to Dan, and bring me a report, that I may know their number." ³ But Joab said, "May the LORD add to his people a hundred times as many as they are! Are they not, my lord the king, all of them my lord's servants? Why then should my lord require this? Why should it be a cause of guilt for Israel?" ⁴ But the king's word prevailed against Joab. So Joab departed and went throughout all Israel and came back to Jerusalem. ⁵ And Joab gave the sum of the numbering of the people to David. In all Israel there were 1,100,000 men who drew the sword, and in Judah 470,000 who drew the sword. ⁶ But he did not include Levi and Benjamin in the numbering, for the king's command was abhorrent to Joab. ⁷ But God was displeased with this thing, and he struck Israel. ⁸ And David said to God, "I have sinned greatly in that I have done this thing. But now, please take away the iniquity of your servant, for I have acted very foolishly." ⁹ And the LORD spoke to Gad, David's seer, saying, ¹⁰ "Go and say to David, 'Thus says the LORD, Three things I offer you; choose one of them, that I may do it to you.'" ¹¹ So Gad came to David and said to him, "Thus says the LORD, 'Choose what you will: ¹² either three years of famine, or three months of devastation by your foes while the sword of your enemies overtakes you, or else three days of the sword of the LORD, pestilence on the land, with the angel of the LORD destroying throughout all the territory of Israel.' Now decide what answer I shall return to him who sent me." ¹³ Then David said to Gad, "I am in great distress. Let me fall into the hand of the LORD, for his mercy is very great, but do not let me fall into the hand of man." ¹⁴ So the LORD sent a pestilence on Israel, and 70,000 men of Israel fell. ¹⁵ And God sent the angel to Jerusalem to destroy it, but as he was about to destroy it, the LORD saw, and he relented from the calamity. And he said to the angel who was working destruction, "It is enough; now stay your hand." And the angel of the LORD was standing by the threshing floor of Ornan the Jebusite. ¹⁶ And David lifted his eyes and saw the angel of the LORD standing between earth and heaven, and in his hand a drawn sword stretched out over Jerusalem. Then David and the elders, clothed in sackcloth, fell upon their faces. ¹⁷ And David said to God, "Was it not I who gave command to number the people? It is I who have sinned and done great evil. But these sheep, what have they done? Please let your hand, O LORD my God, be against me and against my father's house. But do not let the plague be on your people."

There must be true conviction of sin that will lead to true recognition in order to confess for cleansing and restoration based on the atonement of Christ.

Now, we are also exhorted to be pure and blameless in order to be prepared for the day of Christ. Paul focused on the "day of Christ." It is all about this day. All preparation is geared at and directed towards this day. What is the day of Christ? It is important to understand this phrase. This is the second time it appears in just this first chapter of Philippians. The other reference is found in Philippians 1:6, "And I am sure of this, that he who began a good work in you will bring it to completion at the day of Jesus Christ."

A book entitled <u>Maranatha</u> by Renald Showers devotes 40 pages to the day of the Lord.

> The day of Christ is a future event. It is imminent and can happen any moment. Just to touch a bit on what Renad E. Showers says in his book while concluding one chapter called the 'concept of the day of the Lord,' "The Day of the Lord refers to God's special

interventions into the course of world events to judge His enemies, accomplish His purpose for history, and thereby demonstrate who He is – the sovereign God of the universe. The Scriptures indicate that the Day of the Lord in the future will be at least twofold in nature and thus will have two phases. First, during the 70th week of Daniel it will be characterized by darkness and a tremendous outpouring of divine wrath upon the world. Second, during the Millennium it will be characterized by light, an outpouring of divine blessing, and the administration of God's rule over the whole world." (Showers, 1995)[2]

So how do you prepare yourself for the day of Christ? As Paul focused on prayer, you do the same. Focus on key characteristics, what is excellent so that you will be pure and blameless and focus on the Day of Christ.

2. Be filled

Phil. 1:11 filled with the fruit of righteousness that comes through Jesus Christ, to the glory and praise of God.

With what is your heart filled? With what <u>should</u> your heart be filled?

i) Be filled with fruit

Philippians 1:10 is a continuation of Philippians 1:9. God doesn't want us to be empty or filled with anything else at the day of Christ except the fruit of righteousness that comes through Jesus Christ. My questions are, "Are you filled? If you are filled, with

---

2. Showers, Renald E. Maranatha Our Lord, Come! The friends of Israel Gospel Ministry, Inc, Bellmawr, New Yersey, 1995, p 38,39.

what are you filled? With what is your heart filled?" There is an easy way to know this. Please look at:

Matthew 12:34 You brood of vipers! How can you speak good, when you are evil? For out of the abundance of the heart the mouth speaks.

Proverbs 14:14 The backslider in heart will be filled with the fruit of his ways, and a good man will be filled with the fruit of his ways.

Proverbs 15:28 The heart of the righteous ponders how to answer, but the mouth of the wicked pours out evil things.

1 Corinthians 2:11 For who knows a person's thoughts except the spirit of that person

Ephesians 5:18 but be filled with the Spirit

Paul exhorts us in Philippians 1:11 to be filled with the fruit of righteousness. This does not come from within man himself. Since the fall, since man sinned in the Garden of Eden, he has distorted the understanding of what righteousness is. God says that all our righteousness is as filthy rags. "We have all become like one who is unclean, and all our righteous deeds are like a polluted garment. We all fade like a leaf, and our iniquities, like the wind, take us away" (Isa. 64:6).

Our righteous deeds cannot take us to God. This is why the Lord Jesus came into this world. Paul, talking about how we can be made righteous, says in Romans 5:19, "For as by the one man's disobedience the many were made sinners, so by the one man's obedience the many will be made righteous." So this is not a product that <u>we</u> can manufacture, but it is divine.

ii) Be filled with the products that come from Jesus Christ

Yes, the fruit of righteousness comes from the Lord Jesus Christ. If He is the resident of your heart and presiding over every aspect of your life, sanctioning every action, and activity, directing every moment and movement of your life then your are truly experiencing the Lordship of Christ. The Lord who is righteous will give you a fruitful life. "He is the source of your life in Christ Jesus, whom God made our wisdom and our righteousness and sanctification and redemption" (1 Cor. 1:30).

Righteousness means "right kind of living." It is right living in the sight of God and not in your imaginations. "Do horses run on rocks? Does one plow there[1] with oxen? But you have turned justice into poison and the fruit of righteousness into wormwood" (Amos 6:12). Please note the statement made here, "righteousness into wormwood." According to the <u>Zondervan Pictorial Encyclopedia of the Bible,</u> wormwood is a plant "which bears masses of small, yellow flowers."[3] In Jordania, alcohol drink is manufactured. According to the Greek, *apsinthos* means "undrinkable."[4] It has a most objectionable taste. For a moment, think of turning the fruit of righteousness into this kind of taste. So you cannot understand righteousness in your terms, but only from the revealed word of God. The Word tells us:"The fruit of the righteous is a tree of life, and whoever captures souls is wise" (Prov. 11:30). This means that you and I are to be winning souls for the Lord Jesus Christ.

3.Tenney Marrill C. General Editor, The Zondervan Pictorial Encyclopedia of the Bible,Regency Reference Library, Grand Rapids, Michigan, 1975, P969.

4. Ibid, P 969.

Let us look little further and note in:

James 3:16-18 [16] For where jealousy and selfish ambition exist, there will be disorder and every vile practice. [17] But the wisdom from above is first pure, then peaceable, gentle, open to reason, full of mercy and good fruits, impartial and sincere. [18] And a harvest of righteousness is sown in peace by those who make peace.

iii) Be filled with a purpose

What is the purpose of being filled with the righteousness that comes through Jesus Christ? It is found in the conclusion of Paul's prayer as he mentions the glory and praise of God. The prayer began in verse 9 and ends in verse 11.

When you are filled with the fruit of righteousness, you are to glorify God and praise Him. You are not seeking your own honor and praise. The day of the Lord can happen <u>any</u> day; He can appear at any time. How are you going to be found? Would you be found glorifying yourself or Him? Please look at the following verses:

1 Corinthians 10:31 So, whether you eat or drink, or whatever you do, do all to the glory of God.

Ephesians 1:6 to the praise of his glorious grace, with which he has blessed us in the Beloved.

Ephesians 1:12 so that we who were the first to hope in Christ might be to the praise of his glory.

Ephesians 1:14 who is the guarantee of our inheritance until we acquire possession of it, to the praise of his glory.

Conclusion: Are you prepared to meet the Lord if He appears today? In what ways are you specifically preparing? Be focused with your method of prayer to abound in love with knowledge and discernment. This will help you to approve what is excellent, in order to be pure and blameless in your life. This is God's way to prepare for the day of Christ. Don't live a shameful life but be filled with the fruit of righteousness in order to glorify God and praise Him.

Chapter 7

Advancement of the Gospel in the Midst of the Adversities of Life

Text: *Philippians 1:12-14 ¹² I want you to know, brothers,that what has happened to me has really served to advance the Gospel, ¹³ so that it has become known throughout the whole imperial guardand to all the rest that my imprisonment is for Christ. ¹⁴ And most of the brothers, having become confident in the Lord by my imprisonment, are much more bold to speak the word without fear.*

Introduction: The Bible speaks of the adversities true believers faced in the first century and how the Gospel spread during that time. There were persecutions, confusions and false doctrines, all contributing to the adverse conditions that resulted in the spread of the Gospel. When we go through similar trials and persecutions, we are reminded that the adversities that come as a result of preaching the Gospel are inevitable.

During a recent phone call to Pastor K.B. Singh in India, I learned that Bro. K.B. was going through great tribulation as he preached the Gospel. But he had also seen tremendous fruit in the midst of the trials and tests. He was persecuted, beaten, humiliated by people, suffering poverty, experiencing tedious travels and confronted by threats against his life, but he was faithful and stood firm for his faith. As a result, he was able to see thousands reached with the Gospel, several churches planted, and hundreds of people baptized.

Advancement of the Gospel in the Midst of the Adversities of Life

The Apostle Paul talks about the advance of the Gospel at a time when everything should have been coming to an end, from a human perspective. His imprisonment did not stop the spread of the Gospel. His difficulties and the restrictions of being in jail did not put an end to the Gospel. But it motivated many to boldly proclaim the Gospel, removing intimidation that could easily have occurred because of the imprisonment of their beloved leader.

We are exhorted to know and experience the "advancement of the Gospel in the midst of adversities in life." There are three facets to this truth:

1. Adversity happens for a purpose
2. Incredible doors open in the midst of adversities
3. Inexhaustible strength from the Holy Spirit takes the Gospel further

Let's consider each of these.

1. Adversity happens for a purpose

Phil. 1: 12 I want you to know, brothers, that what has happened to me has really served to advance the Gospel

Can any good come out of bad? Have you ever wondered why certain bad things happen or happen to you? Have you ever wondered why certain injustices have been done against you? Are you ashamed because of the humiliation and disgrace of certain past happenings? Please consider the illustrations that follow.

Reflect on the trial of Joseph in the Old Testament.

Genesis 37:12-28[12] Now his brothers went to pasture their father's flock near Shechem. [13] And Israel said to Joseph, "Are not your brothers pasturing the flock at Shechem? Come, I will send you to them." And he said to him, "Here I am." [14] So he said to him, "Go now, see if it is well with your brothers and with the flock, and bring me word." So he sent him from the Valley of Hebron, and he came to Shechem. [15] And a man found him wandering in the fields. And the man asked him, "What are you seeking?" [16] "I am seeking my brothers," he said. "Tell me, please, where they are pasturing the flock." [17] And the man said, "They have gone away, for I heard them say, 'Let us go to Dothan.'" So Joseph went after his brothers and found them at Dothan. [18] They saw him from afar, and before he came near to them they conspired against him to kill him. [19] They said to one another, "Here comes this dreamer. [20] Come now, let us kill him and throw him into one of the pits. Then we will say that a fierce animal has devoured him, and we will see what will become of his dreams." [21] But when Reuben heard it, he rescued him out of their hands, saying, "Let us not take his life." [22] And Reuben said to them, "Shed no blood; cast him into this pit here in the wilderness, but do not lay a hand on him"- that he might rescue him out of their hand to restore him to his father. [23] So when Joseph came to his brothers, they stripped him of his robe, the robe of many colors that he wore. [24] And they took him and cast him into a pit. The pit was empty; there was no water in it. [25] Then they sat down to eat. And looking up they saw a caravan of Ishmaelites coming from Gilead, with their camels bearing gum, balm, and myrrh, on their way to carry it down to Egypt. [26] Then Judah said to his brothers, "What profit is it if we kill our brother and conceal his blood? ²⁷ Come, let us sell him to the Ishmaelites, and let not our hand be upon him, for he is our brother, our own flesh." And his brothers listened to him. ²⁸ Then Midianite traders passed by. And they drew Joseph up and lifted him out of the pit, and sold him to the Ishmaelites for twenty shekels of silver. They took Joseph to Egypt.

Yes, a lot of bad things happened to Joseph from a human perspective, but what does he say about these bad experiences?

Genesis 50:19-21¹⁹ But Joseph said to them, "Do not fear, for am I in the place of God? ²⁰As for you, you meant evil against me, but God meant it for good, to bring it about that many people should be kept alive, as they are today. ²¹ So do not fear; I will provide for you and your little ones." Thus he comforted them and spoke kindly to them.

Now consider this example from the New Testament. "But though we had already suffered and been treated at Philippi, as you know, we had boldness in our God to declare to you the Gospel of God in the midst of much conflict" (1 Thess. 2:2).

How do you respond to the trials that come along in your life? In the history of Israel there were all kinds of trials; some were even the result of their own sin. For example, please look at Lamentations 5:1-3, "Remember, O LORD, what has befallen us; look, and see our disgrace! Our inheritance has been turned over to strangers, our homes to foreigners. We have become orphans, fatherless; our mothers are like widows."

Paul wanted the believers at Philippi to "know" about the events that had happened. The word used here is γινώσκω which means to "know, have knowledge of, find out, learn, understand, perceive, discern, to have knowledge, acknowledge or recognize."

What is he referring to here? Well, let us look at the context of this verse. "For it has been granted to you that for the sake of Christ you should not only believe in him but also suffer for his sake" (Phil. 1:29). Paul was talking about his sufferings and imprisonment so obviously he was referring to the events that led to his imprisonment. But he was not discouraged by these events because he saw a purpose in all of these.

Likewise, in the Old Testament, Joseph saw God's purpose in all the evil that happened to him.

> **Genesis 50:15-20** [15] When Joseph's brothers saw that their father was dead, they said, "It may be that Joseph will hate us and pay us back for all the evil that we did to him." [16] So they sent a message to Joseph, saying, "Your father gave this command before he died, [17] 'Say to Joseph, Please forgive the transgression of your brothers and their sin, because they did evil to you.' And now, please forgive the transgression of the servants of the God of your father." Joseph wept when they spoke to him. [18] His brothers also came and fell down before him and said, "Behold, we are your servants." [19] But Joseph said to them, "Do not fear, for am I in the place of God? [20] As for you, you meant evil against me, but God meant it for good, to bring it about that many people should be kept alive, as they are today.

Advancement of the Gospel in the Midst of the Adversities of Life

Now, let's consider what Paul says in Romans 8:28: "And we know that for those who love God all things work together for good, for those who are called according to his purpose."

Paul had a proper theology which enabled him to understand the things of God. He recognized the purpose of God in all that happened in his life. Paul understood that there was a furtherance of the Gospel; the events that took place were no doubt apparent "obstacles" but they actually contributed to advancement of the Gospel.

Paul was arrested in Jerusalem (Acts 21) and was put in prison in Caesarea (Acts 23-24). This was the providence of God, including the place where Paul was imprisoned, the time he spent in the prison and "the Praetorium of Herod," which all led to the furtherance of the Gospel "Though out the whole praetorian guard"(v 13). Keeping the context in view Hendriksen says, "According to the most natural interpretation it indicates the imperial guard, nine thousand in number, which was instituted by Augusts" (Hendriksen, 1962)[1] Hendriksen further points out to the fact saying, "It is exactly at Rome that the apostle would be constantly guarded by a soldier from this guard and because it rotated, the reason why this remarkble man was imprisoned would gradually become known "throughout the whole praetorian guard and to all the rest."[2]

---

1. Hendriksen William, New Testament Commentary, Baker Books, Grand Rapids, Michigan, 1962, p24.

2. Ibid, P 24.

2. Incredible doors opened in the midst of adversities

Phil. 1:13 so that it has become known throughout the whole imperial guard and to all the rest that my imprisonment is for Christ.

People who are truly called to preach take risks. Paul was a man called to preach and he is a model to us, even today. We read in Acts 9:15-16: "But the Lord said to him, 'Go, for he is a chosen instrument of mine to carry my name before the Gentiles and kings and the children of Israel. For I will show him how much he must suffer for the sake of my name."

While it is not the case that adversities such as imprisonment will come to everyone, if they do come, that believer should never compromise or seek to escape to a "comfortable place."

Note that preaching is not stopped by adverse circumstances. Here in the prison where Paul is, his high ranking guards, the imperial guards, have heard the Gospel. We learn more about this from the following:

> When Paul was arrested in Jerusalem (Acts 21) and shut away in prison in Caesarea (Acts 23-24), one couild easily imagine that this was the end of his ministry, especially as his imprisonment dragged on month after month (Acts 24:27). But in the providence of God both the place of his imprisonment, the Praetorium of Herod (Acts 23:35), and the length of his imprisonment served to thrust the gospel up into higher levels of Roman society than it had ever reached before. Roman military officers, chiliarchs, and centurions (Acts 23:24, 26), as well as Roman soldiers, heard the gospel in Jerusalem

and Caesarea. Two Roman governs, Felix and Fetus along with King Herod Agrippa and their wives heard Paul speak about faith in Christ Jesus (Acts 24:24-27; 25:1-26:32). One of these governors, over a span of two years, often sent for Paul to converse with him (Acts 24:26). News of this celebrated prisoner and his teaching must have spread through the Praetorium, the barracks, and out into the surrounding community. Thus, what appeared at first to be the fatal blow to the Christian mission, the arrest of Paul, turned out to be the means of its revitalization, the key to preaching the gospel before governors and kings (cf Mark 13:9) and their staff personnel. It became evident, therefore, to those in all parts of the residence of the provincial governor of Caesarea "(throughout the entire praetorium)" and to all outside it (to everyone else) that Paul was a prisoner because he was a Christian[3]

The Lord allows us go through certain adverse circumstances, not to abandon us or discourage us, but to fulfill His divine purposes. It was this way in the history of God's people and it still happens this way today. Don't give up in the day of adversity but keep preaching the Gospel. Preach in the hospitals, preach in the prisons, and preach in difficulties. Preach all the time. Never give up! Preaching in adverse circumstances bring positive results. Paul was not silent in his imprisonment. He continued preaching to everyone, as we see in Acts 28:17, 23, 30. Not only did he preach to the guards but also to others in the city as they learned of Paul's imprisonment.

---

3. Martin, P Ralph "Word Biblical Commentary Vol 43 (Revised Edition), Nelson Reference & Electronic Thomas Nelson Publishers, 2004, P44

For Paul, it was not preaching in word only, but in action as well. People around him would watch his inner loyalty, convictions, authority, fearlessness and uncompromising life. All this was a reflection of what he was preaching. Paul preached both in good times and in bad times. What happened in the lives around him will be seen in the next consideration of the advancement of the Gospel in the midst of adverse circumstances in life.

3. Inexhaustible strength from the Holy Spirit takes the Gospel further

Phil. 1:14 And most of the brothers, having become confident in the Lord by my imprisonment, are much more bold to speak the word without fear

These believers were not shaken in spite of all the events that happened to Paul. How about you? Would you run away if your leader was imprisoned for the sake of the Gospel? Does fear grip you that you too may suffer loss if you preach the Gospel?

Please look at Philippians 1:14 which says "most of the brothers" that means not all are included in this increased confidence. These believers were from Rome and were Gentiles. According to Acts 28:24, Paul preached to the Jews when he arrived at Rome. This resulted in churches being planted by the Jews who believed. So there were both Jewish and Gentile believers.[4] When Paul addressed these believers as ἀδελφῶν it

---

4. Hendriksen, William "New Testament Commentary Galations, Ephesians, Philippians, Colossians and Philemon," Baker books, MI, 1968, P69,70.

becomes clear that there was a bond of fellowship between these two groups of believers.[5]

Imprisonment didn't shake the believers or cause them to be timid. The Lord enabled the believers to overcome these adversities in life and He does the same for us today. How did Paul have the strength he had to go through this traumatic time? We see in Acts 23:11, "The following night the Lord stood by him and said, 'Take courage, for as you have testified to the facts about me in Jerusalem, so you must testify also in Rome.' "Yes, it was the Lord who gave him strength and the people around him saw it. MacArthur comments, "As they saw how God protected him and blessed his ministry, despite persecution and imprisonment, their courage was renewed and their boldness and zeal intensified."[6] This gave them confidence as well.

The believers in Rome were bold to preach the Gospel. But boldness didn't come because of intellect; it came by the Holy Spirit. "For God gave us a spirit not of fear but of power and love and self-control" (2 Tim. 1:7).

Consider this illustration from the early church. The early church faced persecution and trials but what kept them going? We're told in Acts 4:31, "And when they had prayed, the place in which they were gathered together was shaken, and they were all filled with the Holy Spirit and continued to speak the word of God with boldness." The first persecution of the church is mentioned in chapter four of Acts but this was certainly not the last. The second is mentioned in chapter 8. Did this stop the spread of the Gospel? No. The early church went on preaching in every circumstance. Please see what happened when persecution

---

5. Ibid P 70
6. MacArthur, John, The MacArthur New Testament Commentary, Philippians, Moody Press, Chicago, ILL 2001, P 63.

scattered the early church believers. It is recorded: "And Saul approved of his execution. And there arose on that day a great persecution against the church in Jerusalem, and they were all scattered throughout the regions of Judea and Samaria, except the apostles" (Acts 8:1). The result: "Now those who were scattered went about preaching the word" (Acts 8:4).

How as this possible? The Holy Spirit is the Spirit of power and He gives supernatural power in times of need. Paul and his team did not go through easy times but they did not give up preaching the Gospel. Please look at:

> **2 Corinthians 4:7-10** [7] But we have this treasure in jars of clay, to show that the surpassing power belongs to God and not to us. [8] We are afflicted in every way, but not crushed; perplexed, but not driven to despair; [9] persecuted, but not forsaken; struck down, but not destroyed; [10] always carrying in the body the death of Jesus, so that the life of Jesus may also be manifested in our bodies.

Conclusion: Are you troubled by trials? Do you feel perplexed and discouraged? Take courage. The Holy Spirit is in you. He can give you supernatural power to go on. The reason you are in this world is to glorify God. There is no better way to glorify God than by bearing abundant fruit. This can happen when you preach the Gospel to others. Keep doing this as a good steward.

Remember that the events and circumstances of your life happen for a purpose. When adversity happens, God opens broader and even more open doors for you to be a witness and He will, by the power of His Spirit, give you inexhaustible strength to preach in those adverse circumstances.

Chapter 8

Examine Your Motives in Preaching the Gospel

Text: *Philippians 1:15-17. ¹⁵ Some indeed preach Christ from envy and rivalry, but others from good will. ¹⁶ The latter do it out of love, knowing that I am put here for the defense of the Gospel. ¹⁷ The former proclaim Christ out of rivalry, not sincerely but thinking to afflict me in my imprisonment*

Introduction: Motives, intentions, nature and attitude are all important when you preach the Gospel. When these are not pure and sincere you will hurt those who are, as Calvin puts it, of "pious" nature. We are living in a day of great challenges. David M. Doran in his book *For the Sake of His Name* quotes Patrick Johnston's estimates on the harvest field.

> Depending on the strictness of the criteria used, we estimate that between 15 % and 25% of the world's population is beyond the reach of the present proclamation of the Gospel. This means that between 800 million and 1,300 million [1.3 billion] people still need to be given their first opportunity to respond to the Gospel.[1]

We also know that there are many who go to church but are not born again. This is very heavy on my heart. People cover themselves with religious masks, cover themselves with ritual

---

1. Doran M. David "For the sake of His Name" Student Global Impact, MI, 2002, P 158, 9.

moisturizers and are content to not have the Gospel actually internalized. In a day like this, if we don't proclaim the Gospel with pure motives, with sincerity and purity, it is very destructive. We know that the Apostle Paul faced a very similar situation.

Perhaps you are thinking this message is not for you because you are not a preacher. Well that is not true. All of us are called to proclaim the Gospel. The great commission is meant for all disciples of Christ. If you are a disciple, then you are to proclaim the Gospel to all people.

We shall look at three aspects that will help you to examine your motives, choose the right motives and drive you to preach the Gospel:

1. Motives that are profane
2. Motives that are pure
3. Motives that you should pursue

Let's examine each of these facets of our motives.

1. Motives that are profane

Phil. 1:15 Some indeed preach Christ from envy and rivalry

What are the profane motives that are prevalent in the lives of people not only in the days of Paul but even today? Profane motives are manifested in many ways. Profane means being irreverent towards holy things.[2] These particular profane

---

2. Vincent, R Marvin "A Cristial and Exegetical Commentary on The Epistles to the Philippians and to Philemon" T & T Clark, Edinburgh, 1897, P 17.

motives were "envy and strife." "Phathonos" is the Greek word for envy and is also used in other places such as "They were filled with all manner of unrighteousness, evil, covetousness, malice. They are full of envy, murder, strife, deceit, maliciousness. They are gossips" (Rom. 1:29).[3]

Please observe the category in which Paul puts people who practice "envy." While he was referring to people who were involved in all kinds of evil, he says they were full of "envy." What I mean to say here is that "envy" belongs to the type of people who are involved in all sorts of wicked things in life. Just imagine if such an evil deed is done by those who are preaching the Gospel? Paul references similar conduct in:

> **Gal. 5:19-21**[19] Now the works of the flesh are evident: sexual immorality, impurity, sensuality, [20] idolatry, sorcery, enmity, strife, jealousy, fits of anger, rivalries, dissensions, divisions, [21] envy, drunkenness, orgies, and things like these. I warn you, as I warned you before, that those who do such things will not inherit the kingdom of God. Here Paul is referring to a group of people who are "walking in the flesh." It is such people who practice "envy" and "strife."

Is Paul criticizing others? No he is plainly telling the truth that others were envious and causing strife. Dr. J. Vernon McGee was a pastor, teacher, author and radio broadcaster who began in 1941. He lectured at a famous Seminary, Dallas Theological Seminary. At the beginning of his ministry, he said it was inconceivable to think that people could preach with envy

---

3. Vincent, R Marvin "A Critical and Exegetical Commentary on The Epistles to the Philippians and to Philemon" T & T Clark, Edinburgh, 1897, P16,7.

and strife. But after years in the ministry, he said there was no other single thing that would be more destructive to the cause of Christ than to see people preaching the Gospel with envy and strife. People are often envious of the good results in the lives of others. *Envy can creep into the mind and heart as you watch people in more influential positions with greater abilities and accomplishments. Envy is sin; don't ever entertain it or allow it to enter you.*

When you preach, you are actually preaching about a Person, the Lord Jesus Christ. We must, therefore, be careful about our motives. What is the Gospel about? It is all about the Lord Jesus Christ.

As I already mentioned, "profane" means to disrespect or be irreverent towards that which is reverent. Similarly, you need to know that when you preach the Gospel, you are actually preaching about the Person of Jesus Christ. This is, therefore, a holy affair. You need to have a holy fear in your heart. So when you preach Christ, He must be the motivating factor to drive you to pure motives. When this happens you are above "envy and strife."What are we to preach? We are to preach Christ! The text says, "Some indeed preach Christ." This implies that some do not! Many people either have a low view or wrong view of Christ.

2. Motives that are pure

If you are truly enlightened by the Lord Jesus Christ you will be ingrained with motives that are pure. Let's examine now what makes for pure motives. Paul says in Philippians 1:15-16: "but others from good will. The latter do it out of love, knowing that I am put here for the defense of the Gospel."

Pure motives are driven by two factors, love and a leader. First, let's look at love. Please look at Philippians 1:16 again: "The latter do it out of love." Yes, love becomes a driving force. It is agape love. We have already observed that agape love reaches out and acts. This agape love is willing to forego self interests and selfish ambitions and to accept sacrifices willingly and voluntarily. Let me illustrate this with a true story from the Old Testament about a man who walked on this very earth on which we live.

> **Genesis 13:1-13** So Abram went up from Egypt, he and his wife and all that he had, and Lot with him, into the Negeb. ² Now Abram was very rich in livestock, in silver, and in gold. ³ And he journeyed on from the Negeb as far as Bethel to the place where his tent had been at the beginning, between Bethel and Ai,⁴ to the place where he had made an **altar** at the first. And there Abram called upon the name of the LORD. ⁵ And Lot, who went with Abram, also had flocks and herds and tents, ⁶ so that the land could not support both of them dwelling together; for their possessions were so great that they could not dwell together, ⁷ and there was **strife** between the herdsmen of Abram's livestock and the herdsmen of Lot's livestock. At that time the Canaanites and the Perizzites were dwelling in the land. ⁸**Then Abram said to Lot, "Let there be no strife between you and me, and between your herdsmen and my herdsmen, for we are kinsmen.**⁹ Is not the whole land before you? Separate yourself from me. If you take the left hand, then I will go to the right, or if you take the right hand, then I will go to the left." ¹⁰ And Lot lifted up his eyes and saw that the JordanValley was well watered everywhere like the garden of the LORD, like the land of Egypt, in the direction of Zoar. (This was

before the LORD destroyed Sodom and Gomorrah.) ¹¹ So Lot chose for himself all the Jordan Valley, and Lot journeyed east. Thus they separated from each other. ¹² Abram settled in the land of Canaan, while Lot settled among the cities of the valley and moved his tent as far as Sodom. ¹³ Now the men of Sodom were wicked, great sinners against the LORD.

The secret of Abraham's sacrificial living could perhaps be tied back to his regular habit of setting up altars. Please see Genesis 12:7-8; 13:4, 8 and 21:9. We understand from the scriptures that an "altar" for the LORD meant there was a sacrifice. "Then Noah built an altar to the LORD and took some of every clean animal and some of every clean bird and offered burnt offerings on the altar" (Gen. 8:20).

If you want to experience love as a driving force in your life so that your motives are pure, you need to sacrifice yourself before His altar. That is where His love is poured into you. Unless you know "sacrifice," you will not know this kind of love. "And walk in love, as Christ loved us and gave himself up for us, a fragrant offering and sacrifice to God" (Eph. 5:2).

Secondly, the leader is your driving force for pure motives in life. Please look at Phil. 1:16 again: "knowing that I am put here for the defense of the Gospel."These people with pure motives were preaching out of love and they knew what was happening to their leader. Their leader was imprisoned for the sake of Gospel. They knew his sincerity and commitment to Christ. They knew that their leader preached the Gospel because of his pure motives and that he was willing to pay the price, even to the extent that he was persecuted. This was a driving force for these believers in Rome. What a challenge it is to observe Paul's life. He is a model for leadership. *He doesn't care about his own comfort and his commitment won't allow him to compromise.*

3. Motives that you should pursue

So what motives should you pursue? What motives should drive your life? "The former proclaim Christ out of rivalry, not sincerely but thinking to afflict me in my imprisonment" (Phil. 1:17).

Are these words written for the sake of "tattling" or complaining or reporting on someone else? Or does Paul have a greater desire than this, to motivate others to pure motives?

What are the motives you pursue? What motives should drive your life? There is a group that is mentioned in our text who do *not* proclaim Christ with pure motives but do so out of strife. They are not sincere in their motives according to Paul. On the other hand, what does Paul said we should pursue? What should drive us? How are we to proclaim the Gospel? He says we are to proclaim the Gospel without rivalry and with sincerity.

Firstly, do not proclaim Christ with strife or rivalry. The word "proclamation" is also used in the sense of advocating, as in Acts 16:21: "They advocate customs that are not lawful for us as Romans to accept or practice" and Acts 17:23: "For as I passed along and observed the objects of your worship, I found also an altar with this inscription, 'To the unknown god.' What therefore you worship as unknown, this I proclaim to you."

The word for strife in Greek is "eris" and it also has the meaning of contention or wrangling. Paul uses the word quarreling in 2 Corinthians 12:20: "For I fear that perhaps when I come I may find you not as I wish, and that you may find me not as you wish - that perhaps there may be quarreling, jealousy, anger, hostility, slander, gossip, conceit, and disorder."

Secondly, Paul says we are to proclaim the Gospel with sincerity. Our actions, plans and purposes will reveal whether we are sincere or whether our motives are selfish. One day God will judge every deed of ours. That day of Christ will show whether our works were sincere or not.

I served the LORD in India from 1975 through 1999 and have seen and met all kinds of people who are serving God in that land. As I traveled across the country I knew hundreds of pastors and Christian leaders. It was painful to watch and hear about those who are in "God's work" to make money for themselves. There is no sincerity.

Conclusion: Examine your motives. Examine yourself to find out what is driving you to serve God. If there were ulterior motives that were profane and destructive to Paul in his days, we can be sure that the same is true for us today. Perhaps you have the same kind of profane motives – motives that are not pure, not resulting from love and sincerity. The answer for this is repentance and then you must pursue the right motives. You need to make a commitment to this. There is no better way to serve Christ than with total dedication.

Chapter 9

Marks of a Positive Life

Text: ***Philippians 1:18-20*** *[18] **What then? Only that in every way, whether in pretense or in truth, Christ is proclaimed, and in that I rejoice. Yes, and I will rejoice,** [19] **for I know that through your prayers and the help of the Spirit of Jesus Christ this will turn out for my deliverance,** [20] **as it is my eager expectation and hope that I will not be at all ashamed, but that with full courage now as always Christ will be honored in my body, whether by life or by death.***

Introduction: Is there any one that has struggled with negative thinking? You say that things are not happening the way they should happen. When we arrived in the United State in 1999, we had struggles that were of different nature but they were still "struggles." I was not used to the things that were around me. For example, I didn't have a car. I felt stranded and dependent. I was so mobile in India having a car that I liked very much, a 118 NE. On top of the struggles that I encountered, I had a most boring job while raising my support. I was helping an sick elderly man. He was unable to walk straight, talk straight and even sleep straight! He needed someone to hold onto for support in order to walk. My job had always been teaching and preaching and here I was stuck as a helpless person helping a helpless man. I was so discouraged and disappointed. But let me tell you something. God has given us new life which means we are resurrected from our old life and in this new life God's supernatural power works every moment of our life and affects our thoughts, our deeds and every single area of our lives. So what do you want in circumstances that are difficult? The supernatural power of God! I went on day after day helping this man and at the same time, I read the Bible to him and preached the Gospel to him the Gospel and prayed with him. I received my regular pay checks and kept pressing on! Meanwhile, we became friends and he began to admire and appreciate me for the comfort he received. *So in the worst circumstances, we have victory because of the supernatural power of God.*

Let me illustrate this with a different kind of story. My son was studying in a Roman Catholic School which was supposed to be one of the top schools in the state. His surroundings were hostile to the Gospel. He had teachers from a different community who would show partiality in grading, the Roman Catholics wouldn't allow the Gospel to be preached or entertain any evangelical witness. This was a very hard time for a Christian boy who wanted to be victorious but the circumstances were so contrary. But, we have great God who answers prayer when situations appear most difficult. My son, Sonu, took his musical instrument to his school. He started playing Christian music. Very soon he became very famous throughout the whole school. Teachers and even the principal surrounded him. A Roman Catholic priest wanted him at the front of the school gatherings every morning. This reached a particular climax. For the first time in the history of this particular Roman Catholic school, at the Christmas celebration, Sonu became the singing and music leader, with Roman Catholic priests all around him, Hindu teachers in the audience and Hindu students singing Christmas carols. What happened was a breakthrough. Sonu never took part in the mass (which was part of the program) but brought the true message of Christmas through songs and music at that occasion.

Trust God and believe Him and you will have a positive outlook and influence in every circumstance of life. Paul faced hard and disappointing circumstances but he had a positive approach and positive influence. I am not suggesting anything like the television guys who preach erroneous theology on positive thinking. I want to bring biblical truths to light on a positive perspective and impact. There are three sure marks of a positive life that are found in Philippians 1:18-20. They are:

1. Determination in disturbances
2. Divine provision for deliverance
3. Daring in disappointments

Let's look at each now in detail.

1. Determination in disturbances

Disturbances are inevitable in our lives according to the Bible but you can have great determination in your heart when you are disturbed in life. We shall see what that our determination should be as we go along. People like Daniel and his friends were people who lived on this very earth with tremendous pressures from all around but they had positive perspective. They never gave up, even when they saw problems like mountains in front of them. Please look at

Daniel 1:5 The king assigned them a daily portion of the food that the king ate, and of the wine that he drank. They were to be educated for three years, and at the end of that time they were to stand before the king.

Daniel 1:8 But Daniel resolved that he would not defile himself with the king's food, or with the wine that he drank. Therefore he asked the chief of the eunuchs to allow him not to defile himself.

Here you have "determination" and commitment not to come under the influence of the heathen country even when there is great political pressure to be defiled. There is no compromise for Daniel. Paul says in Philippians 1:18: "What then? Only that in every way, whether in pretense or in truth, Christ is proclaimed, and in that I rejoice. Yes, and I will rejoice."

What were the "disturbances" in Paul's life? There were people preaching the Gospel from pretense. Paul was determined, though, to "rejoice," even in spite of and contrary to human reasoning. Humanly speaking it was genuinely disturbing. The people around Paul were preaching for reasons that were not right.

We've already seen that there were many preaching the Gospel with profane motives; they were preaching with envy and strife. People can be envious of good results in others' lives. Remember what we said...*Envy can creep into your mind and heart as you watch people in more influential positions with greater abilities and accomplishments. Envy is sin. Don't ever entertain it and allow it to enter you.* You'll remember that "profane" means to disrespect or be irreverent toward reverent issues.

Now, Paul goes on to say, "What then?" Commentator William Hendriksen interprets this as "what really matters?" Christ is being preached and people hear the good message and may not even notice the motives that are inside of people. So whatever the case is, Christ is preached and therefore Paul has a reason to rejoice. Paul mentions rejoicing seven times in the book of Philippians (1:18 - two times, 2:17, 18, 28, 3:1, and 4:4 two times). Consider what Paul says in

Philippians 2:16-18[16] holding fast to the word of life, so that in the day of Christ I may be proud that I did not run in vain or labor in vain. [17] Even if I am to be poured out as a drink offering upon the sacrificial offering of your faith, I am glad and rejoice with you all. [18] Likewise you also should be glad and rejoice with me.

Paul rejoices in the fact that Christ is preached. Now Christ is a person. He is God and the Gospel is about Him who came down to this world to lay down His life. The story doesn't end at the cross but He is resurrected from the dead. Paul encountered this resurrected Christ. Remember "Last of all, as to one untimely born, he appeared also to me" (1 Cor. 15:8). So Paul rejoices over this fact that Christ is proclaimed.

2. Divine provision for deliverance

Phil. 1:19 I know that through your prayers and the help of the Spirit of Jesus Christ this will turn out for my deliverance

There is a divine provision for deliverance for every believer. There are lots of remedies that are available today, but they are not all divine. For example:

- Think of Oprah Winfrey and all that she offers to people. She is connected with a person that teaches a "New Age Jesus;" Oprah believes that Jesus is not the only way to God.

- Think of Yoga. This is talked about as physical exercise but it is not. It is the central teaching of Bhagwat Gita and talks of five steps of spiritual experience that conclude in the culmination with Brahma. Be very careful of these teachings.

- Think of the New Age Movement. A new religious expert named J. Gordon Melton says that New Age "is ultimately a vision of a world transformed, a heaven on Earth, a society in which the problems of today are overcome and new existence emerges."

- Think of gurus who come from the east and teach people how to breathe. Well they go beyond teaching on breathing because they teach about the spiritual side of life.

And then there are people who with their teachings talk about deliverance. Hank Hanegraaff mentioned recently that he had dinner with a famous faith healer who is on TV. Hank said to him, "You claim that thousands of people are healed, give me three evidences of real healing." This faith healer gave him three evidences and all three were bogus. These people and many others are seeking to experience deliverance from difficult circumstances and have confidence about the future. When Paul talks about his future and his deliverance, he says, "for I know that through your prayers and the help of the Spirit of Jesus Christ this will turn out for my deliverance" (Phil. 1:19). Paul talks about the prayers of God's people and the power of God's Spirit. This is how he knows of his secure future and his deliverance.

Firstly, Paul speaks of the prayers of God's people. Calvin says, "For he who depends for help on the prayers of the saints relies on the promise of God."

What is that provision you experience when you need deliverance from a particular circumstance or problem? Do you turn to God's people and ask them to pray? I have many prayer requests that need prayer and I also have a burden to pray for them. I stop my work and look to the Lord in prayer. Then, I turn to others asking for their prayers on my behalf. We are interdependent. In the preceding verses Paul talked about his prayer for the Philippians and here he is asking others to pray for him. This is humility in action because even though he is a leader, he still asks other believers to pray. Do you ask others to pray for your specific needs?

Prayer is God's divine provision for deliverance. Prayer must be based on God's word and not based on experience. Experience can be absolutely wrong and misleading and not all experiences are based on God's word. Consider the examples of people who were diligent in prayer, such as George Muller, Hudson Taylor, Bakth Singh, A.W. Tozer and others.

Secondly, Paul is confident about his deliverance and future because of the power of God's Spirit. Calvin appropriately puts it when he says that "the supply of God's Spirit is the efficient cause and prayer is a subordinate help."[1] He says the Spirit pours into us everything of which we are destitute and prayer is "employed to mean the furnishing of what is wanting."[2]

Through the prayers of God's people and the supply of God's Spirit there will be deliverance. The supply of God's Spirit in a believer's life is a wonderful provision from God in order to be strong in the time of trouble and experience deliverance. God's Spirit has not only sealed us but is a guarantee that we will be safe until the end. "And it is God who establishes us with you in Christ, and has anointed us, and who has also put his seal on us and given us his Spirit in our hearts as

---

1. Calvin, John, Calvins Commentaries Vol XXI, Baker Book House, Grand Rapids, Michigan, P 40.

2. Ibid, p 40.

a guarantee" (2 Cor. 1:21-22). "He who has prepared us for this very thing is God, who has given us the Spirit as a guarantee. So we are always of good courage" (2 Cor. 5:5-6).

In Philippians 1:19, the Greek word "soteria" means "salvation." In other places, Paul uses this word as a reference to the ultimate salvation that a believer would experience. (Rom. 1:16; 10:10; 13:11; 2 Cor. 7:1; 1 Thess. 5:8-9; 2 Thess. 2:13). Many interpreters insist that Paul is talking about himself, that he would endure until the end and be saved. But there is also another meaning for "soteria" which refers to welfare or health. So certain interpreters think that Paul is referring to his vindication from the court. I believe that according to the context, Paul is talking about his deliverance from his immediate circumstances and being delivered from imprisonment. These were not only Paul's sufferings but also the sufferings of others, as they were affected by Paul's sufferings.

Paul had his disappointments. He was humiliated, imprisoned and shut off from normal life but he never gave up on his commitment keep going for the Lord. He already said, "And I am sure of this, that he who began a good work in you will bring it to completion at the day of Jesus Christ" (Phil. 1:6).

3. Daring in disappointments

Phil.1:20 as it is my eager expectation and hope that I will not be at all ashamed, but that with full courage now as always Christ will be honored in my body, whether by life or by death.

Who are the most daring people in the world? They are not the Al-Qaidaor those who would use nuclear weapons. These people are, in fact, the most timid people because they don't know how to face challenges in life.

Marks of a Positive Life

The third mark of a person who lives with positive perspective on life is that he is daring in disappointments because of God's provision. There is a three-fold approach for a positive perspective in a time of disappointments. These three are:

- One anticipation
- One attribute
- One ambition

Paul talks here about not being ashamed. The word "ashamed" is to be understood in its proper sense. This is not taking "shame" or "insult" upon yourself. Scholar James Montgomery Boice says that a biblical understanding shame has to do with disappointment. In Romans 5:5 Paul used the word καταισχύνω which means "put to shame, humiliate, disgrace, disappoint."English translations use "ashamed." To understand this clearly, it means hope will not disappoint us. Please look at another reference:

> **Isaiah 49:23** Kings shall be your foster fathers, and their queens your nursing mothers. With their faces to the ground they shall bow down to you, and lick the dust of your feet. Then you will know that I am the LORD; those who wait for me shall not be put to shame.

Paul's anticipation was that he would not be disappointed! What was Paul's one attribute in this time of disappointment? He was full of courage. This is supernatural power working in his life. I have always said in my preaching that Paul had absolutely untainted theology and that helps me to think, talk and walk straight. For example, please look at

Romans 8:11-15 [11] If the Spirit of him who raised Jesus from the dead dwells in you, he who raised Christ Jesus from the dead will also give life to your mortal bodies through his Spirit who dwells in you. [12] So then, brothers, we are debtors, not to the flesh, to live according to the flesh. [13] For if you live according to the flesh you will die, but if by the Spirit you put to death the deeds of the body, you will live. [14] For all who are led by the Spirit of God are sons of God. [15] For you did not receive the spirit of slavery to fall back into fear, but you have received the Spirit of adoption as sons, by whom we cry, "Abba! Father!"

This new life enables every believer who is truly committed to Him to glorify Him no matter the cost and to live this bold and courageous life. Paul says, "For God gave us a spirit not of fear but of power and love and self-control" (2 Tim. 1:7). Paul had one attribute in a situation like this; he was courageous. This allowed him to be daring in the face of disappointments.

Thirdly, Paul had one ambition. What was it? At any cost, he would glorify God, come what may, whether by death or by life! Later on he did die as a martyr. What a glorious death. A brave soldier of Christ, once killing others who believed in Christ, but now dedicated to glorify only Christ! He laid down his life for the cause of the cross. Are you ready for such a life? Is your church ready for such a life? We don't die to escape our responsibility but we die for the sake of cross. Paul's desire was that Christ be magnified in his body.

Romans 8:37-39 [37] No, in all these things we are more than conquerors through him who loved us. [38] For I am sure that neither death nor life, nor angels nor rulers, nor things present nor things to come, nor powers, [39] nor height nor depth, nor anything else in all creation, will be able to separate us from the love of God in Christ Jesus our Lord.

Conclusion: Do you desire to have a positive perspective and impact in life? The Bible has the answers. Your commitment to Christ will determine your perspective. For example, if you are committed to the Lord in all circumstances, you will determine to be a part of Sunday fellowship, no matter the time of day. In the introduction, I mentioned my struggles when I came to the United States and Sonu's challenges in school. Now listen to this true story of Emmanuel Emmady. When he first came to the United States, he did not have car. What would he do on Sundays? He walked two miles every Sunday. Not just one Sunday but Sunday after Sunday after Sunday for 12 to 16 Sundays. That was a true test of his commitment and he passed. Such lives are victorious and courageous.

Chapter 10

Features of Your Life on Earth

Text: *Philippians 1:21-26* ²¹ *For to me to live is Christ, and to die is gain.* ²² *If I am to live in the flesh, that means fruitful labor for me. Yet which I shall choose I cannot tell.* ²³ *I am hard pressed between the two. My desire is to depart and be with Christ, for that is far better.* ²⁴ *But to remain in the flesh is more necessary on your account.*²⁵ *Convinced of this, I know that I will remain and continue with you all, for your progress and joy in the faith,* ²⁶ *so that in me you may have ample cause to glory in Christ Jesus, because of my coming to you again*

Introduction: I would like you to read this chapter with two questions in mind.

1. What is the purpose of my life on this earth?
2. How do I explain to myself and others what the purpose of my life on this earth is?

From our passage, we shall learn what features should characterize your life and how to live your life on this earth to display these features.

1. Live for Christ while you live on the earth
2. Labor for the progress of the church while you live on the earth
3. Long for your departure to be in the same place as Christ while you live on the earth in order

Features of Your Life on Earth

There is a song that shows where your real home is if you're a Christian and how you should feel while you live on this earth. Listen to a portion of the lyrics from *This World is Not My Home:*

> *This world is not my home, I'm just passing through.*
> *My treasures are laid up somewhere beyond the blue.*
> *The angels beckon me from Heaven's open door*
> *And I can't feel at home in this world anymore.*

Recently my son got an upgraded phone for my wife (and plans to do the same for me). He gave us the choice to select the phones. We looked at the costs as well as the phone features. The same is true of the spiritual realm. We must look at the price or cost while we considers the features in life or what life has to offer.

So you need to consider the features of your transient life on this earth. As long as the Lord keeps you on this earth, what features should characterize your life?

1. Live for Christ while you live on the earth

Phil. 1:21 For to me to live is Christ, and to die is gain.

"Live" in Greek is "zein" and is in the continuous form (while "death" or "die" is one time act). Paul is talking about his life and death on this earth. There is one life and one death on this earth. He was determined that he would live as a testimony to Christ and that death would be a triumph.

Firstly, he would live as a testimony to Christ. Please listen to these words of Paul from:

> **2 Corinthians 5:15-20** [15] and <u>he died</u> for all, that those who live might no longer live for themselves but <u>for him who for their sake died and was raised.</u>[16] From now on, therefore, we regard no one according to the flesh. Even though we once regarded Christ according to the flesh,

we regard him thus no longer. ¹⁷ Therefore, if anyone is <u>in Christ</u>, he is a new creation. The old has passed away; behold, the new has come. ¹⁸ All this is from God, who <u>through Christ reconciled</u> us to himself and gave us the ministry of reconciliation; ¹⁹ that is, <u>in Christ God was reconciling</u>¹ the world to himself, not counting their trespasses against them, and entrusting to us the message of reconciliation. ²⁰ Therefore, we are <u>ambassadors for Christ</u>, God making his appeal through us. We implore you <u>on behalf of Christ</u>, be reconciled to God.

Please notice seven observations about Christ:

1. He died
2. But for Him who for their sake died and was raised
3. In Christ
4. Through Christ, reconciled
5. In Christ, God was reconciling
6. Ambassadors for Christ
7. On behalf of Christ

Paul's hero was Christ. When you have a hero in your life, you always want to talk about him. I have real heroes in my life and I talk about them. Their names keep popping up in my preaching. I love them and take great pleasure in talking about them. The Apostle Paul talks about Christ very often. He describes Him, loves Him and cherishes Him. Christ transformed His life. You like to talk about a person who has done great things in your life. For example, look at the above scripture passage and you'll notice how much is said about Christ in such a short text.

How much time do you take to speak for Him, about Him and to Him? Who is the subject of your worship? Who is the subject of your daily devotion? Who is the subject of your daily walk in life? Who is the subject of your talk?

Secondly, death would be triumph. Now, please listen to Paul's words as he writes in:

1 Corinthians 15:54-57 [54] When the perishable puts on the imperishable, and the mortal puts on immortality, then shall come to pass the saying that is written: "Death is swallowed up in victory." [55] "O death, where is your victory? O death, where is your sting?" [56] The sting of death is sin, and the power of sin is the law. [57] But thanks be to God, who gives us the victory through our Lord Jesus Christ. 2 Timothy 4:7-8. [7] I have fought the good fight, I have finished the race, I have kept the faith. [8] Henceforth there is laid up for me the crown of righteousness, which the Lord, the righteous judge, will award to me on that Day, and not only to me but also to all who have loved his appearing.

Does 2 Timothy 4:7-8 flash into your mind when you see someone passing away in front of you? This once happened to me.

2 Tim. 4:7-8 [7]I have fought the good fight, I have finished the course, I have kept the faith; [8]in the future there is laid up for me the crown of righteousness, which the Lord, the righteous Judge, will award to me on that day; and not only to me, but also to all who have loved His appearing.

Are you living a life that is a good fight of faith? That means that when you encounter trials, you do so with joy. "Count it all joy, my brothers, when you meet trials of various kinds, for you know that the testing of your faith produces steadfastness" (Jas. 1:2-3)."In all circumstances take up the shield of faith, with which you can extinguish all the flaming darts of the evil one" (Eph. 6:16).

Paul says to die is gain. Death is gain to a believer because of all that is in store for life after death. Paul knew his eschatology very well which is why he was able to talk about his death so triumphantly. Consider Paul's own words: "For this slight momentary affliction is preparing for us an eternal weight of glory beyond all comparison, [18] as we look not to the things that are seen but to the things that are unseen. For the things that are seen are transient, but the things that are unseen are eternal" (2 Cor. 4:17-18).

Now consider Philippians. 1:21 again, please: "For to me to live is Christ, and to die is gain." To live is a testimony because you are living to testify of the person of Jesus Christ. Life is worth living for Him every moment. Your values for life on the earth are a real expression of the person for whom you are living. To die is gain because you know your theology well, that you are going to inherit all that glory, elevated position, crown, mansion, security, triumph, no pain, no sorrow and all that is for eternity and all of these cost you nothing. Jesus bought it all. Can you say, "Hallelujah!"?

2. Labor for the progress of the church while you live on the earth

Until the day you die you have something to do and what is that?

Phil. 1:22-26 [22] If I am to live in the flesh, that means fruitful labor for me. Yet which I shall choose I cannot tell. [24] But to remain in the flesh is more necessary on your account.[25] Convinced of this, I know that I will remain and continue with you all, for your progress and joy in the faith,[26] so that in me you may have ample cause to glory in Christ Jesus, because of my coming to you again.

Is Paul talking to individuals? Yes, but he is talking to the corporate body as well. How do we know this? The context determines this. Please look at Philippians 1:1: "To all the saints in Christ Jesus who are at Philippi, with the overseers and deacons." These saints are the church as it says in Philippians 4:15: "And you Philippians yourselves know that in the beginning of the Gospel, when I left Macedonia, no church entered into partnership with me in giving and receiving, except you only."

What contributes to the progress of the church? There are two aspects that will help us to understand further: fruitful labor is for the progress for the church and a fervent desire to labor is for the progress of the church.

Firstly, fruitful labor is for the progress of the church. "If I am to live in the flesh, that means fruitful labor for me" (Phil. 1:22). Paul is talking about his earthly life. The Greek word σάρξ, σαρκός means flesh, physical body, or human nature. Here, in this context, he is talking about his life on this earth. We shall look at couple of other references to understand how the word "labor" is used. Please look at:

> **Mark 13:33-34** [33] Be on guard, keep awake. For you do not know when the time will come. [34] It is like a man going on a journey, when he leaves home and puts his servants in charge, each with his work, and commands the doorkeeper to stay awake.

Here it is used in the sense that we need to be working with great alert. Now, let consider another place where the same Greek word is employed. "Jesus said to them, 'My food is to do the will of him who sent me and to accomplish his work' "(John 4:34).You are not working for the sake of working or an attitude of "it doesn't matter" but you are actually doing the very will of God. This is how the Lord Jesus Christ worked. So it is a labor that means being alert and doing the will of God. But Paul also mentions specifically the group of people whose progress he is working to see. Paul is working for the progress of the local church. This is a model for you and me. How are you using your life? C.T. Studd said, "Only one life, 'twill soon be past, only what's done for Christ will last."

Secondly, we are to have a fervent desire to labor for the progress of the church.

Phil. 1:22b-26 ...Yet which I shall choose I cannot tell. ²³But I am hard-pressed from both directions, having the desire to depart and be with Christ, for that is very much better;²⁴ But to remain in the flesh is more necessary on your account.²⁵ Convinced of this, I know that I will remain and continue with you all, for your progress and joy in the faith, ²⁶ so that in me you may have ample cause to glory in Christ Jesus, because of my coming to you again."

Paul's fervent desire was to serve the church at Philippi if he was to remain in the flesh. He was willing to go back to the Philippians once he was out of prison. If Paul's life on earth could bring progress and joy in the faith, it must not be any different for you and me. You, too, by investing your life on earth can bring progress and joy in the faith for the people of the church. Please notice that progress and joy in the faith go together. You need progress as well as joy. For many people, neither are found in life. Yet there are people who may have progress in life but there is no joy in the faith. "Though you have not seen him, you love him. Though you do not now see him, you believe in him and rejoice with joy that is inexpressible and filled with glory" (1 Pet. 1:8).When I think of this verse I think of Brother Bakth Singh of India. He wrote his testimony in a small booklet called *How I Received Joy Unspeakable Full of Glory*. All the way to the end of his life, he was a powerful witness as he lived to give others progress and joy in the faith. His life was dedicated to God to live for the progress and joy of people in the church.

So we labor for the progress of the church. Until the time you die, you have a task to accomplish. If you are not faithful, you will one day experience the tragedy expressed in song, "Must I go with empty hands, must I meet my savior so?"

So win souls and bring them to the Lord. Invest your time, money and energy for the progress of God's people in the church and for their joy in the faith. But remember that there should also be a longing to depart and be with the Lord.

3. Long for your departure in order to be in the same place as Christ while you live on the earth

Phil. 1:23 I am hard pressed between the two. My desire is to depart and be with Christ, for that is far better.

Have you ever had a dilemma in making decisions in your life? Paul did. His dilemma was between staying back on earth and going to his eternal dwelling place. He had a longing for and desire to depart and be with Christ in his eternal dwelling place.

Firstly, there was a desire for departure. The Greek word used here comes from the root word $αναλυω$ which means to unloose, to depart. It is used here for departing from life. Paul used the same word in 2 Timothy 4:6: "For I am already being poured out as a drink offering, and the time of my departure has come." Have you ever prayed that the Lord would show you your end and prepare you for your end? Moses prayed like this:

> **Psalm 90:6-12** [6] in the morning it flourishes and is renewed; in the evening it fades and withers. [7] For we are brought to an end by your anger; by your wrath we are dismayed. [8] You have set our iniquities before you, our secret sins in the light of your presence. [9] For all our days pass away under your wrath; we bring our years to an end like a sigh. [10] The years of our life are seventy, or even by reason of strength eighty; yet their span is but toil and trouble; they are soon gone, and we fly away. [11] Who considers the power of your anger, and your wrath according to the fear of you? [12] So teach us to number our days that we may get a heart of wisdom.

The word for "desire" is very intense because it means "lust" or "longing." That was the nature of his desire to depart from this life. This was not a desire to get rid of responsibilities on this earth but a desire to depart so that he could be in a better place. What is that place?

Secondly, there was a desire for a dwelling place. Here is the understanding about what happens after death. The believer will go to the place where the Lord Jesus Christ is right now. This means your dwelling will be plucked out from this earth and put in the very presence of the Lord Jesus Christ. That is why our bodies are known as "tents." This means we are in a transient place. The permanent place is the place where Christ is right now. The Apostle Peter tells us, "I think it right, as long as I am in this body, to stir you up by way of reminder, since I know that the putting off of my body will be soon as our Lord Jesus Christ made clear to me" (2 Pet. 1:13-14).

The Greek word that is used for "body" is $\sigma\kappa\epsilon\iota\nu\omega\mu\alpha$ and the literal meaning of this word is tabernacle or tent. Let us remember the words of the Lord in John 14:3: "And if I go and prepare a place for you, I will come again and will take you to myself, that where I am you may be also." You must make sure that before departing from this life you are going to be with Christ for your eternal dwelling.

While working on this chapter, I have been going through an interesting experience with respect to my health. When I went to see the doctor, my blood pressures was taken and it was 88/56. I have never had such a low blood pressure in all my life. It was like sinking and departing from this earth. But the Lord kept me on. I drove back home safely and the next day, I began to have pain in the chest, a constant pain and didn't know what it was. But it was a good reminder that I could depart from this physical body at any time.

Conclusion: Our lives are short, as Moses the man of God prayed and observed. So as long as you are on this earth, live for Christ, labor for the progress of the church and for joy in the faith of the people of God and remember that you will depart one day, so long for your departure to be in the place where Christ is now.

Chapter 11

Manner of a Life that is Worthy of the Gospel

Text: *Philippians 1:27-30* ²⁷ *Only let your manner of life be worthy of the Gospel of Christ, so that whether I come and see you or am absent, I may hear of you that you are standing firm in one spirit, with one mind striving side by side for the faith of the Gospel,* ²⁸ *and not frightened in anything by your opponents. This is a clear sign to them of their destruction, but of your salvation, and that from God.* ²⁹ *For it has been granted to you that for the sake of Christ you should not only believe in him but also suffer for his sake,* ³⁰ *engaged in the same conflict that you saw I had and now hear that I still have.*

Introduction: The Bible doesn't permit us to live in whatever way we choose, though this is exactly what we have tried to do. It says in Isaiah 53:6: "All we like sheep have gone astray; we have turned every one to his own way; and the LORD has laid on him the iniquity of us all."

There is a great transformation that takes place in every life which has truly experienced God's redemption. We are not only saved from our sins and the wrath of God but we are brought into a relationship with God that brings us under one authority. The Apostle Peter says in 1 Peter 2:24-25: "He himself bore our sins in his body on the tree, that we might die to sin and live to righteousness. By his wounds you have been healed. For you were straying like sheep, but have now returned to the Shepherd and Overseer of your souls."

So this removes any confusion about what kind of life I should lead on this earth. We are given clear direction on how to live. All this is found in the Bible. The Apostle Paul talks about the manner of life in the text that is before us. What is supposed to be the manner of our lives?

The manner of life that is worthy of the Gospel has three facets. It includes:

- The experience of standing: Philippians 1:27
- The experience of salvation: Philippians 1:28
- The experience of suffering: Philippians 1:29-30

Please look at the text again, Philippians 1:27-30, and see how each verse is connected but there is a closer connection between verses 29 and 30. We will look at verses 27 and 28 separately and take verses 29 and 30 together.

All Scripture is given for us to experience. We are exhorted to stand firm and this can happen only when we walk worthy of the Gospel. But there are opponents around us that try to stop us from standing firm. We need to know that we don't have to be frightened because of our salvation from God. The sufferings that we face during our time on earth are actually allowed by God.

1. The experience of standing

Phil. 1:27 Only let your manner of life be worthy of the Gospel of Christ, so that whether I come and see you or am absent, I may hear of you that you are standing firm in one spirit, with one mind striving side by side for the faith of the Gospel

There are two aspects of standing. They are 1) standing for the sake of the Gospel and 2) standing together for the faith of the Gospel. Firstly, we are to stand for the sake of the Gospel. Paul says, "Only let your manner of life be worthy of the Gospel of Christ, so that whether I come and see you or am absent, I may hear of you that you are standing firm" (Phil. 1:27).

This new section begins with a transitional word "monon" which means "only." Paul's great concern was how the believers of Philippi would live. Whether he was present or absent, visited them or not, he wanted their lives to be worthy of a special cause and that cause is the Gospel of Christ. Please note that "Gospel" is mentioned two times in the same verse. It is worth understanding what the Gospel is in order to live a life worthy of it and in order to stand firm for it.

What is the Gospel? The Word of God has the answer.

      a.   It is the Gospel of God: Romans 1:1
      b.   It is the Gospel of Christ: Phil 1:27
      c.   It is the Power of God: Romans 1:16
      d.   It is the grace of God: Acts 20:24
      e.   It is the Gospel of Salvation: Ephesians 1:13
      f.   It is the Gospel of peace: Ephesians 6:15
      g.   It is the glorious Gospel: 2 Corinthians 4:4

When you have a proper understanding of the Gospel, you desire to walk worthy of it and as you walk worthy of it, you are standing. Standing speaks of strength. You are not stumbling but standing. If you have ever watched a little child learning to stand, you understand the difference between stumbling and standing. I see this in my own granddaughter as she is learning to stand.

Secondly, stand together for the faith of the Gospel. Paul says that we are "standing firm in one spirit, with one mind striving side by side for the faith of the Gospel" (Phil. 1:28). Is there some motivation that will help you to stand in life?

Romans 14:4 Who are you to pass judgment on the servant of another? It is before his own master that he stands or falls. And he will be upheld, for the Lord is able to make him stand.

Galatians 5:1 For freedom Christ has set us free; stand firm therefore, and do not submit again to a yoke of slavery.

2 Thessalonians 2:15 So then, brothers, stand firm and hold to the traditions that you were taught by us, either by our spoken word or by our letter.

1 Corinthians 16:13 Be watchful, stand firm in the faith, act like men, be strong.

Paul exhorts the Philippians to stand with one mind, striving side by side for the faith of the Gospel. The Gospel is the motivating factor for you to stand. How do you stand? Paul says we stand with one spirit, with one mind, striving together. We must have a proper understanding of the Gospel and then we must live a life that is worthy of the Gospel so that we will stand in one spirit, with one mind, striving together. This will help you to be fearless of opponents and to have an assurance from God of your salvation.

2. The experience of salvation

Phil. 1:28 and not frightened in anything by your opponents. This is a clear sign to them of their destruction, but of your salvation, and that from God.

Consider two key aspects of the experience of salvation. We are able to 1) live a fearless life because of our salvation and 2) live a fortified life because our salvation is from God. Firstly, we are to be fearless because of salvation. Paul talks about not fearing his opponents because one day these opponents will be destroyed but the believers will be saved. One commentator observes that Paul says "your" salvation meaning that salvation is personally and individually possessed by the believers of Philippi. What is this salvation? Please look at Ephesians 2:8-9: "For by grace you have been saved through faith. And this is not your own doing; it is the gift of God, not a result of works, so that no one may boast" and Romans 10:9-10: "because, if you confess with your mouth that Jesus is Lord and believe in your heart that God raised him from the dead, you will be saved. For with the heart one believes and is justified, and with the mouth one confesses and is saved."

Every true believer possesses this salvation; therefore every believer should have the assurance of this salvation. This assurance protects the believer from every kind of fear, even fear of opponents. Who are these opponents who may scare us? Please look at Philippians 1:15: "Some indeed preach Christ from envy and rivalry" and Philippians 3:18-19: "For many, of whom I have often told you and now tell you even with tears, walk as enemies of the cross of Christ. Their end is destruction, their god is their belly, and they glory in their shame, with minds set on earthly things."

The end of the enemies of the cross is destruction but for true believers, it is salvation. This is one sure reason why believers should be fearless. The Lord protects us each day and one day, this salvation will be complete as the apostle says in 1 Peter 1:5: "...who by God's power are being guarded through faith for a salvation ready to be revealed in the last time."

- What are some of the fears that come, even to believers?
- Fear of humiliation
- Fear of falling
- Fear of loosing (reputation, health, wealth, influence, leadership, people etc)
- Fear of persecution
- Fear of being put aside (sidelined)

Secondly, we are to live a fortified life because our salvation is from God. The problem with many people is that they don't have a biblical or growing understanding of God. Their lives are shallow. "...but the people who know their God shall stand firm and take action" (Dan. 11:32).

Paul doesn't just talk about salvation but he says it is from God. This is the same God who has taken away wrath, the God who can save from the fire, the God who can deliver one from prison, the God who can bring fire from heaven, the God who is a consuming fire, the God who loves with an everlasting love and who is mighty in deeds! This "experience of salvation" isn't just an experience, but it involves trust in God for His salvation and waiting for future salvation.

3. The experience of suffering

Phil. 1:29-30 [29] For it has been granted to you that for the sake of Christ you should not only believe in him but also suffer for his sake, ³⁰ engaged in the same conflict that you saw I had and now hear that I still have.

There are two components of suffering. Paul is referring to 1) sufferings that are associated with our belief in Christ and 2) sufferings that are associated with being the servant of Christ.

Let's look first at the sufferings that are associated with our belief in Christ. There is a close association, a relationship and a connection that is inseparable between the true believer and the sufferings of Christ. "Then they left the presence of the council, rejoicing that they were counted worthy to suffer dishonor for the name" (Acts 5:41). "…that I may know him and the power of his resurrection, and may share his sufferings, becoming like him in his death" (Phil. 3:10).

You will be amazed at the number of times the Apostle Peter refers to the sufferings of Christ in his first epistle. Peter exhorts the believers in the area of suffering.

1 Peter 1:11 inquiring what person or time the Spirit of Christ in them was indicating when he predicted the sufferings of Christ and the subsequent glories.

1 Peter 2:21-23 ²¹For to this you have been called, because Christ also suffered for you, leaving you an example, so that you might follow in his steps. ²² He committed no sin, neither was deceit found in his mouth. ²³ When he was reviled, he did not revile in return; when he suffered, he did not threaten, but continued entrusting himself to him who judges justly.

1 Peter 3:18 For Christ also suffered1 once for sins, the righteous for the unrighteous, that he might bring us to God, being put to death in the flesh but made alive in the spirit,

1 Peter 4:1 Since therefore Christ suffered in the flesh,1 arm yourselves with the same way of thinking, for whoever has suffered in the flesh has ceased from sin,

1 Peter 4:13 But rejoice insofar as you share Christ's sufferings, that you may also rejoice and be glad when his glory is revealed.

1 Peter 5:1 So I exhort the elders among you, as a fellow elder and a witness of the sufferings of Christ, as well as a partaker in the glory that is going to be revealed:

1 Peter 5:10 And after you have suffered a little while, the God of all grace, who has called you to his eternal glory in Christ, will himself restore, confirm, strengthen, and establish you.

So the scriptures teach what it means to be associated with the sufferings of Christ. Secondly, there are sufferings that are associated with being the servant of Christ. Paul says in Philippians 1:30: "…engaged in the same conflict that you saw I had and now hear that I still have." We often think that we are alone in what we are undergoing. No, it is not true. We go through sufferings that God's other servants go through too.

Conclusion: Transformation through the Word of God is imperative. We are to walk worthy of the Gospel by standing firm in one spirit, being of one mind and striving together for the faith of the Gospel with an assurance of experiencing salvation and being partakers of the sufferings of Christ.

Chapter 12

Appeal for Unity – Part I

Text: *Philippians 2:1-4*[1] *So if there is any encouragement in Christ, any comfort from love, any participation in the Spirit, any affection and sympathy,* [2] *complete my joy by being of the same mind, having the same love, being in full accord and of one mind.* [3] *Do nothing from rivalry or conceit, but in humility count others more significant than yourselves.* [4] *Let each of you look not only to his own interests, but also to the interests of others.*

Introduction: As we've already seen, the church at Philippi had people from different backgrounds, as churches often do. Because of this, the church is a very good place to practice unity. It is also good preparation for eternity, since heaven will include people from all nations, languages and backgrounds. Satan knows this very well and will do whatever he can to bring "disunity' among God's people. People can divide over doctrine, language, region or some particularly minor issues.

Consider this true story that took place in Dallas, Texas. The congregation was divided and the division became so serious that each faction sued the other to disassociate the church from the other party and to claim the church property for itself. This litigation was reported in the newspapers and many people watched the court proceedings with great interest. In fact, it was reported in the newspaper for all of Dallas to read that the court, in tracing this squabble to its source, found that the trouble began when an elder at a church dinner received a smaller slice of ham than the child seated next to him![1]

There were problems of disunity in the first century church and there are problems of the same kind today. This is because the devil is active. Our text is not only relevant and appropriate to the church at Philippi but to the church today.

Scholars such as Martin Lloyd Jones ("The Apostle here is making his great appeal for unity")[2] and Moises Silva ("Paul once again addresses the issue of the Philippians' unity as the one matter that concerns him')[3] believe that Paul was appealing for unity here. Paul pled that they would make his joy complete and the only way to accomplish this was by the unity of the believers. It is interesting to remember that Paul was in prison, was facing a significant trial and was going through very difficult circumstances. Yet, he was not thinking of his own interests but appealed to the church at Philippi to stay united because that would cause Paul's joy to overflow. Dwight Pentecost says there are four propositions in this text,[4] as does Lightfoot. Donald Guthrie says these are common features to every believer and to unity. The resources for unity are:

---

1. Pentecost, J. Dwight, The Joy of Living, Kregel Publications, Grand Rapids, Michigan, 1973, p 57

2. Lloyd-Jones, D. Martin, The Life of Joy An exposition of Philippians 1 and 2, Baker Book House, Grand Rapids, Michigan, 1989, P 135.

3. Silva, Moises The Wycliffe Exegetical Commentary Phlippians,Moody Press, Chicago Ill, 1988, P 100.

4. Pentecost, J. Dwight, The Joy of Living, Kregel Publications, Grand Rapids, Michigan, 1973,P57.

Appeal for Unity – Part I

1. Encouragement in Christ
2. Comfort from love
3. Participation in the Spirit
4. Affection and sympathy

The verse needs to be read like this: *If there is any encouragement, if there is any comfort from love, if there is any participation in the Spirit and if there is any affection and sympathy, then…*Paul goes on to give instructions or commands about maintaining unity. What are these instructions, these commands?

1. Be of the same mind
2. Have the same love
3. Be in full accord
4. Be of one mind

If you want to have unity, you must know the four resources for unity and the four commands or instructions for unity. The four resources are already in the believer's possession and the four instructions or commands must be obeyed by every believer.

1. Encouragement in Christ

Phil. 2:1 So if there is any encouragement in Christ

There is a connection between these verses and the preceding text. The verse begins with "Therefore" or "So." Look back at Philippians 1:27: "Only let your manner of life be worthy of the Gospel of Christ, so that whether I come and see you or am absent, I may hear of you that you are standing firm in one spirit, with one mind striving side by side for the faith of the Gospel."

Paul had been exhorting the believers to walk worthy of the Gospel and to stand firm in one spirit with one mind for the sake of the Gospel. Different scholars believe that the word here is "exhortation." One scholar, Lightfoot,[5] says that the subject of the sentence is an exhortation for unity; the Greek word *paraklesis* should be translated "exhortation." Therefore, the verse reads, "If there is any exhortation in Christ..." Another scholar, Peter T. O' Brien,[6] says that there is a wealth of meanings for this word such as exhortation, encouragement, appeal, request, comfort, consolation.

The word "if" is mentioned in rhetorical form. Paul does not doubt here. Is there any exhortation in Christ? The answer is a definitive, "Yes!" Our relationship with Christ is strengthened by the exhortation or encouragement that we receive from God's Word. Our knowledge of God is an exhortation in our lives. My question to you today is, "Are you open to God's exhortation or God's encouragement in your life?" Please don't forget what we have heard from chapter one of Philippians, especially the last section from verse 27 through the end of the chapter. Exhortation is a great resource from God to keep us going on in life. Are you exhorting your spouse, another member in the family, members in the local church, and members in the body of Christ? If so, in what way are you encouraging others? Sometimes it takes a rebuke, sometimes a gentle word, sometimes hospitality but whatever the case may be, everything must be supported by the Word of God.

---

5. Lightfoot, J.B., St. Paul's Epistle to the Philippians, A revised Text with Introduction n Nores and Dissertations, Zondervan Publishing House, Grand Rapids, Michigan, first printing 1953, P 107.

6. O'Brien, Peter. T., The Epistle to the Philippians, A commentary on the Greek Text, William B. Eerdmans publishing company, Grand Rapids, Michigan, 1991, P 167.

2. Comfort from love

Do believers have the comfort that comes from love? The answer is, "Yes!" When you possess God, you also possess love. The Greek words are παραμύθιον ἀγάπης. Here is Christian love. Is there any comfort from love? The answer is, "Yes!" According to one scholar, Peter O'Brien, "The basic sense of the verb in classical Greek was 'to speak to someone in a friendly way.' " This love refers to Christ's love. Do you have Christ's love reigning in you now? If not, why not? If you don't have the love of God in you, you are leading a disobedient life. This is a divine resource that every believer possesses.

3. Participation in the Spirit

The third resource is participation in the Spirit. This refers to the Holy Spirit. This is another great resource that every believer possesses. The moment you believe in Christ, you have the Holy Spirit indwelling in you.

Ephesians 1:13 In him you also, when you heard the word of truth, the Gospel of your salvation, and believed in him, were sealed with the promised Holy Spirit

Romans 8:16 The Spirit himself bears witness with our spirit that we are children of God

Romans 8:14 For all who are led by the Spirit of God are sons of God.

4. Affection and sympathy

The Greek words are σπλάγχνα καὶ οἰκτιρμοί. The fourth resource is affection and sympathy. These two qualities could be two branches of the same tree. Paul exhorts the Colossian believers to put on certain qualities and these two qualities are found in that list. "Put on then, as God's chosen ones, holy and beloved, compassion, kindness, humility, meekness, and patience" (Col. 3:12).

The word σπλάγχνον, refers to one's inmost self or feelings, heart. It also refers to affection, love (διὰ ς. ἐλέους θεοῦ because of God's tender mercy Luke 1:78); οἰκτιρμός, οὗ compassion, mercy, and pity.

So there are four resources: encouragement in Christ, comfort from love, participation in the Spirit and affection and sympathy. Montogomery Boice says these are four solid legs that the Christian has for unity. (Boice, 1971)[7] These four resources are given for a purpose and that purpose is to have unity. Having these four resources, possessing them as ours, we will now look at four commands we need to obey in life.

1. Be of the same mind

Firstly, to experience unity you need to have the same mind. Having the same mind doesn't mean coming under some pressure from external forces. It is not being influenced by some incentives. But it is an inner drive that comes because of the four resources that we have just seen. Is it possible to have same mind? There is only one way it is made possible. Please look at Philippians 2:5: "Have this mind among yourselves, which is yours in Christ Jesus."

---

7. Montgomery Boice, James, Philippians An expostional Commentary, Baker Books, Grand Rapids, Michigan, 1971,2000, P 98.

Appeal for Unity – Part I

To have the mind of Christ is to have His humility, His love, His compassion, His affection, His purity, His Spirit and such. The Bible exhorts us to put on Christ, meaning to clothe ourselves with Him. Consider the following verses:

Romans 12:16 Live in harmony with one another. Do not be haughty, but associate with the lowly.

Never be conceited. The word used here is φρονέw. We are to think, to have in mind (φ. τά with general, think the thoughts of, have one's mind controlled by; τὸ αὐτὸ φ. or ἕν φ. live in harmony of mind, agree with one another; ὑψηλὰ φ. be proud, have proud thoughts); care for, be concerned about (τὸ φρονεῖν concern, care, Phil. 4.10); think highly of (Rom. 14.6a).

1 Corinthians 1:10 I appeal to you, brothers, by the name of our Lord Jesus Christ, that all of you agree and that there be no divisions among you, but that you be united in the same mind and the same judgment.

1 Peter 3:8 Finally, all of you, have unity of mind, sympathy, brotherly love, a tender heart, and a humble mind.

2. Have the same love

Secondly, we are commanded to have the same love. There is only one kind of love that God gives. This is divine love that is produced by the Holy Spirit. This love should reflect biblical love. It should be:

- Sacrificial love: This is how the Lord loved us. The Bible exhorts us to follow His example.

- Supporting love: Is your love supportive, to lifts others up?
- Sincere love: Love is not self-seeking but sincere, which is reflected in attitude, motives, daily walk, talk, etc.

The New American Standard Bible translates Philippians 2:2 in this way: "Make my joy complete by being of the same mind, maintaining the same love, united in spirit, intent on one purpose."

3. Be in full accord (or united in spirit)

The word here, σύμψυχος, ον, means united in spirit, as one. Here is a good example from the early church:

Acts 1:14 All these with one accord were devoting themselves to prayer, together with the women and Mary the mother of Jesus, and his brothers.

Acts 2:1 When the day of Pentecost arrived, they were all together in one place.

Acts 2:46 And day by day, attending the temple together and breaking bread in their homes, they received their food with glad and generous hearts

Acts 4:24 And when they heard it, they lifted their voices together to God and said, "Sovereign Lord, who made the heaven and the earth and the sea and everything in them

4. Be of one mind

On what were they supposed to be of one mind? They were to be of one mind in their intention, their purpose and their goal!

Appeal for Unity – Part I

Listen to the prayer of our Lord just before His death:"that they may all be one, just as you, Father, are in me, and I in you, that they also may be in us, so that the world may believe that you have sent me" (John 17:21).

Conclusion: We are exhorted to live in unity. This is possible because we have four resources. Those resources are: exhortation, comfort from love, participation in the Spirit, and being of one mind. We also have four clear commands regarding unity. We are commanded to be of the same mind, have the same love, be in full accord and be of one mind.

Chapter 13

Appeal for Unity - Part II

Text: *Philippians 2:1-4 So if there is any encouragement in Christ, any comfort from love, any participation in the Spirit, any affection and sympathy, ^{2} complete my joy by being of the same mind, having the same love, being in full accord and of one mind. ^{3} Do nothing from rivalry or conceit, but in humility count others more significant than yourselves. ^{4} Let each of you look not only to his own interests, but also to the interests of others.*

Introduction: In the last chapter, we looked at verses 1 and 2. In Part II, we will look at verses 3 and 4. There are so many things that happen in our world that are competitive. Think of people in sports, the arts or with various talents. People are competitive. To the people of the world, this brings rivalry. There is rivalry among people to prove one person is better than another. This has taken hold of our culture and has crept into the church and Christian work. How sad!

Paul has a message and that message is relevant and practical for today. What I hear from the work in India troubles me greatly. Christian leaders have become competitive and work as rivals against each other. These people get money from the west and use it to commercialize Christian work. Christian leaders are buying Christian workers from other churches and organizations by offering to pay them more money. They say, "We will pay you more; come and join our work." In spite of living in a day like this, is it possible to live with a good testimony, working in humility and sincerity.

Let me illustrate with a personal story. I worked in one local church for 17 of the 23 years I served in North India. The Lord taught me great lessons there. He taught me what true submission is and what it means to humble one's self and be under leadership. I had to pay the price for this. The credit for what I did must go to the senior pastor for his conduct, example and leadership. I could easily draw people's attention to myself but that would bring disunity and I needed to guard against it. I could have accused the senior pastor for the wrong things that I thought I saw in his life but I needed to be careful and guard myself because of what Scripture says. I remember David not touching Saul, the king of Israel, the Lord's anointed. I soon discovered that people around me in the church and city began to like me and I had a good, responsive audience around me. There was a temptation to overtake the senior pastor or bypass him. This would not have honored Christ, nor was it Christ-like. I needed to submit to the Lord in all practical areas of life. There could have been a division in the church but the Lord helped it not to happen.

I believe with all my heart that true unity is possible and this needs to be practiced in your local church, in your home, in your organization and everywhere that God has placed you. Are you ready? Let us look at the text to find out measures that will help us.

The second part of the text is: Phiippians 2: 3-4:"Do nothing from rivalry or conceit, but in humility count others more significant than yourselves. Let each of you look not only to his own interests, but also to the interests of others."

There are four truths by which a believer must live in order to maintain unity. They are:

1. Rivalry and conceit destroy unity
2. Regarding others builds unity
3. Self-interest destroys unity
4. Regarding the interests of the saints builds unity

Let us look at these in detail.

1. Rivalry and conceit destroy unity

We must look a bit at this text in terms of the original writings. In Greek, there is no verb. Philippians 2:3 μηδὲν κατ' ἐριθείαν μηδὲ κατὰ κενοδοξίαν But to give a clear understanding of the text in English, the translation says, "DO NOTHING."Do nothing from a heart of rivalry and conceit.

We already are acquainted with the word rivalry from Philippians 1:15. The word used here in verse 3 is ἐριθεία, which means selfishness, selfish rivalry and selfish ambition. Selfishness is an enemy of the spiritual life and opposes all unity. The only way to live a Spirit-filled life is through the cross of Christ. "I have been crucified with Christ. It is no longer I who live, but Christ who lives in me. And the life I now live in the flesh I live by faith in the Son of God, who loved me and gave himself for me" (Gal. 2:20).

Paul didn't just have an intellectual knowledge of the cross but a practical knowledge as well. Many people know about the cross but have no personal experience of it. In order to have a practical experience with the cross of Christ, we must take all of "self" to the cross and nail it there through our humble submission to His divine authority and divine Lordship. This kind of submission has no reservation or argument. It is an absolute. In the Bible, "self" is identical with the flesh. Please look at:

> **Romans 8:5-9** [5] For those who live according to the flesh set their minds on the things of the flesh, but those who live according to the Spirit set their minds on the things of the Spirit. [6] To set the mind on the flesh is death, but to set the mind on the Spirit is life and peace. [7] For the mind that is set on the flesh is hostile to God, for it does not submit to God's law; indeed, it cannot. [8] Those who are in the flesh cannot please God. [9] You, however, are not in the flesh but in the Spirit, if in fact the Spirit of God dwells in you. Anyone who does not have the Spirit of Christ does not belong to him.

Paul uses the same word εριθια in Romans 2:8: "but for those who are self-seeking and do not obey the truth, but obey unrighteousness, there will be wrath and fury."

In Philippians 1, we saw that we should not have profane motives in preaching the Gospel but pure motives. Here in the second chapter we are again reminded to serve God by doing nothing from a heart of rivalry or conceit. The word for conceit is κενοδοξια, which means a cheap desire to boast. It also means foolish fancy or vain glory. The Bible exhorts us to do everything for God's glory, not our own. "So, whether you eat or drink, or whatever you do, do all to the glory of God" (1 Cor. 10:31).

2. Regarding others builds unity

Phil. 2:3b but in humility count others more significant than yourselves.

Are others significant in your life? If so, how are they significant? We are to have humility, then we are to make others more significant than ourselves.

Paul uses the same word ταπεινοφροσύνη in Acts 20:19: "serving the Lord with all humility and with tears and with trials that happened to me through the plots of the Jews..."Peter also uses this wordin1 Peter 5:5: "Likewise, you who are younger, be subject to the elders. Clothe yourselves, all of you, with humility toward one another, for God opposes the proud but gives grace to the humble."

What is humility? Here's what it is not!

- It is not wearing a mask because that is hypocrisy
- It is not an acting phony; it must come from the heart of "original quality"
- It is not acting like something you are not; for example, if your six feet tall, don't make yourself 4 1/2 feet tall. That is not humility.
- It is not false weakness that makes you to give in everything for lack of strength. Biblical humility is a spiritual quality of a Spirit-filled believer.

But humility is:

- When others are recognized and you rejoice in God
- When others are preferred and you praise God
- When others are called and you celebrate in God
- When others are selected and you are secure in God
- When you are rejected and you do not rebel
- When you are denied and you overcome being disturbed in soul

Appeal for Unity – Part II

- When you are ignored and you are not intimidated
- When you are appreciated and you adore God in response
- When you are respected and you revere God

This is the humility that recognizes others as better than yourself.

3. Self-interest destroys unity

Phil. 2: 4 Let each of you look not only to his own interests

The believer must overcome self interests. We are prone to promote the interests of our own families, our own churches and our own communities. What does "self interest" look like:

- Personal gain at the cost of others – stepping on others to achieve your goal is wrong!
- Personal laughter at the cost of others – making fun or hurting others to make a joke or get a laugh is wrong!
- Personal glamour which is self-centered – overlooking the need of others because you will lose your glamour in life is wrong!

We are required to live for others in obedience to the following exhortations:

Ephesians 4:25-30 ^{25}let each one of you speak the truth with his neighbor, for we are members one of another. ^{26} Be angry and do not sin; do not let the sun go down on your anger, ^{27}and give no opportunity to the devil. ^{28} Let the thief no longer steal, but rather let him labor, doing honest work with his own hands, so that he may have something to share with anyone in need. ^{29} Let no corrupting talk come out of your mouths, but only such as is good for building up, as fits the occasion, that it may give grace to those who hear. ³⁰ And do not grieve the Holy Spirit of God, by whom you were sealed for the day of redemption.

Ephesians 4:32 Be kind to one another, tenderhearted, forgiving one another, as God in Christ forgave you.

Colossians 3:12-14 ¹² Put on then, as God's chosen ones, holy and beloved, compassion, kindness, humility, meekness, and patience, ¹³ bearing with one another and, if one has a complaint against another, forgiving each other; as the Lord has forgiven you, so you also must forgive. ¹⁴ And above all these put on love, which binds everything together in perfect harmony.

Hebrews 12:14 Strive for peace with everyone, and for the holiness without which no one will see the Lord.

4. Regarding the interests of the saints builds unity

Phil. 2:4 but also to the interests of others

"Others" refers to the saints about whom Paul speaks in Phil. 1:1. What are the interests of others? First, regarding the "interests of others" has to do with their spiritual welfare. This includes such things as:

- Making phone calls to others and showing your interest in others
- Meeting others in person to help in some practical way
- Motivating others to live godly lives in practical areas
- Mobilizing others for witnessing and being an example yourself

Second, regarding the "interests of others" has to do with your spiritual witness. Don't do anything that can destroy your witness for the Lord, whether in your marriage, your job, on the internet, in your friendships, etc. Here are some other considerations:

- The testimony of family members is important as God's witnesses. This includes your "earthly" family and your church family. When we take part in the Lord's Table, we are reminded from the Scriptures that there is ONE BODY and ONE CUP, meaning Christ's body is not divided. This is our testimony.
- Triumph over situations that are unhealthy; this is imperative for the sake of being God's witnesses.
- Tell others about Christ by your life and words; how you live and the words you speak are interrelated.

Conclusion: During this past week, I received an email from a Christian leader in England who said that there has been a division in Pakistan among a particular assembly. This is a warning to us. These assemblies were made up of faithful prayer warriors who had a powerful witness. How sad it is to see disunity among such churches!

Are you personally working toward unity in the body of Christ? Give up any thing that has to do with rivalry or conceit. Look to the interests of others. Be practically involved in helping others. Regard others as more significant, more important than you. Look to the interests of other saints in the family and the church.

Chapter 14

Have the Mind of Christ

Text: *Philippians 2:5-8* ^{5} *Have this mind among yourselves, which is yours in Christ Jesus,* ^{6} *who, though he was in the form of God, did not count equality with God a thing to be grasped,* ^{7} *but made himself nothing, taking the form of a servant, being born in the likeness of men.* ^{8} *And being found in human form, he humbled himself by becoming obedient to the point of death, even death on a cross.*

Introduction: God knows us because He made us. He knows our feelings, our attitudes, our temperaments and our behavior. Nothing is hidden from Him because of His omniscience (all-knowing) and omnipresence (being present everywhere). He is present everywhere and knows everything. He knows everything that goes on in the minds of people. As recorded in Genesis 11, there was a time when people came together and began to build a tall tower for the wrong reasons. God changed their plan by scattering these people everywhere on the earth. The building stopped and God's plan prevailed.

In the New Testament we notice that there is a coming together of people and this coming together was for a good purpose. God was not against it, but for it. He wanted this togetherness. In the previous chapter, we looked at unity. God wants unity in His body. And God knew that there could not be unity among His people unless they were of one mind. Now whose mind is the best to have so that we can have one mind?

Have the Mind of Christ

Would it be Dr. Billy Graham? If we all have the mind of Billy Graham, we would probably think of preaching to the whole world. What about the mind of Neil Armstrong? If we all had the mind of Neil Armstrong, we would love to go to the moon. But the Bible says there is no one who is perfect on this earth. When Solomon built his great temple, he prayed these words, "If they sin against you - for there is no one who does not sin" (I Kngs 8:46).

So if there is no one who is sinless and perfect, whose mind should we have? Paul gives us the answer in Philippians 2:5. We are to have the mind of Christ! What does it mean to have the mind of Christ? There are two components to having the mind of Christ. We must understand the command given to a particular community and the cost paid by Christ.

There are many commandments in the New Testament that a believer is required to obey. In Philippians 2:5, Paul gives a commandment to a particular group of people. Then in the verses that follow, Paul explains the cost paid by our Lord as an act of His humility. Let us look at these in detail.

1. The command given to a particular community

The command given in Phil**ippians 2:5** is to have this mind among yourselves, which is yours in Christ Jesus. There are two aspects to this command. First, the command to have "the mind of Christ" is given only to a particular community and second, the command is to have *only* the mind of Christ. Let's look at the first aspect of this command. It focuses on the community or group of people to whom the commandment is given. While the commandment to repent from sins in order to be born into the family of the Lord is for all people, the commandment to walk with Him is given only to His children. You can only walk with

Him after being born. One must first be born into the family of God (John 3:3 and John 1:12) and then you can start walking with Him. Consider Ephesians 5:8: "for at one time you were darkness, but now you are light in the Lord. Walk as children of light."

Paul said, "Have this mind among yourselves." "Yourselves" refers to the called, the "saints" mentioned in Philippians 1:1. Let us look at another synonym for saints. In 1 Peter 2:9, Peter says it this way: "But you are a chosen race, a royal priesthood, a holy nation, a people for his own possession."

These saints are a:
- Chosen race
- Royal priesthood
- Holy nation
- People of His own possession

That is a beautiful description of the community of God's people. The commandment to have the mind of Christ is given to this community.

The second aspect focuses our attention on having *only* the mind of Christ. Why should we have only the mind of Christ and not the mind of others? Please look at what Paul is saying in:

> **2 Corinthians 5:13-15** ^{13}For if we are beside ourselves, it is for God; if we are in our right mind, it is for you. ^{14}For the love of Christ controls us, because we have concluded this: that one has died for all, therefore all have died; and he died for all, that those who live might no longer live for themselves but for him who for their sake died and was raised.

Here is what we need to understand. The Lord had transformed and changed the mind of Paul. The transformation came through the love of Christ. The motivation for his mind to be different from what he was before Christ was "the love of Christ." It is because of the love of Christ that every believer must have the mind of Christ. Basically everyone is selfish because of the absence of true love. But when you accept Christ, your life is changed and you begin to love everyone.

Consider this true illustration from the life of Billy Graham. Somehow, in even the most difficult situations, Billy Graham communicates a heart full of love for others. People sense it. His internalizing love has deepened through the years as he has listened intently to the Spirit, whose first fruit the Bible says is love. In an article from *Christian Century*, Billy Graham explained what had been happening to him after a decade of international ministry.

"I am now aware that the family of God contains people of various ethnological, cultural, class, and denominational differences. ... Within the true church there is a mysterious unity that overrides all divisive factors. In groups which in my ignorant piousness I formerly "frowned upon," I have found men so dedicated to Christ and so in love with the Truth that I have felt unworthy to be in their presence. I have learned that although Christians do not always agree, they can disagree agreeably, and that what is most needed today is for us to show an unbelieving world that we love one another."

In his meetings, Billy Graham has often asserted, "God is saying to you, 'I love you. I love you. I love you.'" His love has been obvious to others and has radiated to his colleagues and those he leads, as well as to the watching world.

Sometimes love is shown by a thoughtful word, by willingness to help an employee in trouble or by refusal to retaliate when attacked. Other times, love is shown by simply showing up.

At the time Billy Graham was in his mid-80s and struggling physically, Leighton and Jean Ford's daughter, Debbie, Billy's niece, had successfully endured cancer treatments but then learned the cancer had recurred. Debbie was apprehensive as she entered the Mayo Clinic in Jacksonville, Florida, for a bone scan.

"I was very fearful of cancer being found somewhere else in my body," Debbie told us. As she walked back to her room, she glanced down the empty hallway. There at the end, sitting in a wheelchair and facing her direction, was a frail older man. She realized it was Uncle Billy, who happened to be at Mayo for some tests. Debbie relayed, "Knowing I was there, he had asked the Mayo staff to locate where I was in the clinic. I ran and threw my arms around him and sobbed with all my heart. He held me tenderly, saying over and over, 'I love you.' When I looked up to tell him how frightened I was, I saw that he was also crying. In his own weakened state, he met me at my weakness."

Debbie was deeply touched by this evidence of Billy Graham's love for her. "Certainly he's a great evangelist and a confidant of leaders," said Debbie. "He's also a tender and frail older man. Despite the fact that he hurts like I do and has concerns for his body like I do, he's thoughtful and caring and willing to take time for me, just as I am."

Listen to the same truth in this quote from Martin Luther King, Jr.: "Whom you would change, you must first love." Why else should we have only the mind of Christ? Because He alone is perfect! "For our sake he made him to be sin who knew no sin, so that in him we might become the righteousness of God" (2 Cor. 5:21).

Everyone else is sinful. Only Christ is exempt from sin. Therefore, we need to have only His mind. The Lord Jesus Christ alone is sinless, He alone is perfect and you can trust Him. If you have His mind, this is what happens:

- **Forgiveness**:

Luke **23:34** And Jesus said, "Father, forgive them, for they know not what they do."And they cast lots to divide his garments.

- **Love in action**:

John 13:4-5 (Jesus) rose from supper. He laid aside his outer garments, and taking a towel, tied it around his waist. ⁵ Then he poured water into a basin and began to wash the disciples' feet and to wipe them with the towel that was wrapped around him.

- **You will not revile**:

1 Peter 2:23 When he was reviled, he did not revile in return; when he suffered, he did not threaten, but continued entrusting himself to him who judges justly.

2. The cost paid by Christ

You can not think of having His mind unless you know the cost He paid. Without this understanding, you will have a superficial Christian life. If you truly desire a deep and meaningful spiritual life, you must comprehend the sacrificial life of Christ.

Phil. 2: 6-8 ⁶who, though he was in the form of God, did not count equality with God a thing to be grasped, ⁷but made himself nothing, taking the form of a servant, being born in the likeness of men. ⁸And being found in human form, he humbled himself by becoming obedient to the point of death, even death on a cross.

Please look at the actions taken by our Lord to deepen your understanding of the "mind of Christ." He:

- Set aside equality with God: The Lord set aside His majesty and glory in heaven

- Made Himself nothing: The Lord became nothing for our sake

- Took the form of servant: This speaks of submission, of being under authority and doing the will of the Father.

- Was born in the likeness of men: He took on a human body to live on this earth. He shed tears. He hungered. He was thirsty and was tired. He was troubled and tempted. He was humiliated and threatened. "Men" is a plural form, translated from the Greek. This is to represent the entire human race.

- Was made in the human form: He faced death as a criminal. His body was broken. He bled.

- Was humbled by obedience: How do you demonstrate your humility? The Lord demonstrated humility by obedience. Obedience manifests true humility.

- Died on the cross: He died openly before everyone. People mocked Him. He was shamed. He carried the sins of the world. When the Bible says to bear one another's burdens, this burden of carrying the sins of the world would be far too great for us!

Isaiah 53:12 Therefore I will divide him a portion with the many, and he shall divide the spoil with the strong, because he poured out his soul to death and was numbered with the transgressors; yet he bore the sin of many, and makes intercession for the transgressors.

Conclusion: If you are born into the family of God, you are part of God's community of people. This commandment to have the mind of Christ is given to you.

Chapter 15

Exaltation Comes from God

Text: *Philippians 2:9-13* *⁹ Therefore God has highly exalted him and bestowed on him the name that is above every name, ¹⁰ so that at the name of Jesus every knee should bow, in heaven and on earth and under the earth, ¹¹ and every tongue confess that Jesus Christ is Lord, to the glory of God the Father.*

The text begins with the word, "Therefore."

We have many examples in the Bible showing us that it is God Who gives promotions, Who moves one forward in life and lifts a person up from the dust. But He does all these in His way and not in our way. Here are few examples:

- Joseph
  God elevated him while people put him down. He was sold into slavery and his character was assassinated. He was put in prison and forgotten by people to whom he had done good. But God worked in His own way and His own time to make him Prime Minister of the country of Egypt.

- David
  God says in **2 Samuel 7:8:** "Now, therefore, thus you shall say to my servant David, 'Thus says the LORD of hosts, I took you from the pasture, from

following the sheep, that you should be prince over my people Israel.' "

- Daniel
  Daniel 6:3: "Then this Daniel became distinguished above all the other presidents and satraps, because an excellent spirit was in him. And the king planned to set him over the whole kingdom." Daniel was under various kings of Babylon who were ungodly. He lived with the pressure of being a captive. Darius was one king who elevated Daniel.

2 Samuel 22:36 You have given me the shield of your salvation, and your gentleness made me great. Yes, God has His way of exaltation and that way is perfect, divine and best.

1. God's way is through humility

Phil. 2:9 Therefore God has highly exalted him and bestowed on him the name that is above every name

The word "therefore" explains how God exalts. God is the subject in the statement here. Yes, it is God who exalts. God chooses to exalt only through humility. "Humble yourselves, therefore, under the mighty hand of God so that at the proper time he may exalt you" (1 Pet. 5:6).

There are so many things of which we may wrongly boast, such as:

- Your face, your race and your pace
- Your job
- Your home
- Your education

Consider Proverbs 8:13: "The fear of the LORD is hatred of evil. Pride and arrogance and the way of evil and perverted speech I hate" and Proverbs 11:2: "When pride comes, then comes disgrace, but with the humble is wisdom."

The ultimate model of true humility is the Lord Jesus Christ. He humbled Himself by becoming obedient, even to the point of death on the cross. That required utter self denial, being willing to be shamed and humiliated by ungodly people. Are you willing for such humiliation in life?

God gives the name that is above every name. There is a definite article before "name." It is *the* name. There is a special significance of this name, Jesus.

Acts 4:12 And there is salvation in no one else, for there is no other name under heaven given among men by which we must be saved.

Acts 4:18 So they called them and charged them not to speak or teach at all in the name of Jesus.

Acts 5:40-41 [40] and when they had called in the apostles, they beat them and charged them not to speak in the name of Jesus, and let them go. [41] Then they left the presence of the council, rejoicing that they were counted worthy to suffer dishonor for the name.

If you want God to lift you, you need to humble yourself. Humility in every area of your life is required. When He allows you to go through humbling circumstances, you must submit to Him because this is God's way and one day you will see that you are elevated.

I have previously shared about my experience on the Logos ship in 1974. I lived on the ship for five months, while going through an intensive leadership training program. The Lord gave me many wonderful experiences. One of them was to take the challenge to do janitorial work. The intensive leadership training included goals such as reading the whole Bible through one time and the entire New Testament twice in the five months on the ship. We were also to memorize three scripture verses a week and do 400 hours of evangelism and 400 hours of manual work in the five months onboard the ship. At one point during those five months, the people who had the responsibility for cleaning the toilets went on vacation. One day it was announced that there would be a need for volunteers to do the janitorial work for a couple of weeks. I took the challenge and said, "I will do that" and I gladly did so for those couple of weeks. What the Lord did was amazing and it proved to be a great gift from the Lord. A door opened to preach in Thailand. The leadership on the Logos ship selected a three-member team and decided that I should be one the three. When this team preached, there was a phenomenal response. Not only did the people hear the Word but the people generously gave financial help as well. It was a great honor from and elevation by the Lord.

2. God's way is for the whole of humanity

Phil. 2:10 so that at the name of Jesus every knee should bow, in heaven and on earth and under the earth

God gave that kind of name for a purpose. Consider the way in which God honored the woman in Mark 14.

Mark 14:3-9 [3] And while he was at Bethany in the house of Simon the leper, as he was reclining at table, a woman came with an alabaster flask of ointment of pure nard, very costly, and she broke the flask and poured it over his head. [4] There were some who said to themselves indignantly, "Why was the ointment wasted like that? [5] For this ointment could have been sold for more than three hundred denarii and given to the poor." And they scolded her. [6] But Jesus said, "Leave her alone. Why do you trouble her? She has done a beautiful thing to me. [7] For you always have the poor with you, and whenever you want, you can do good for them. But you will not always have me. [8] She has done what she could; she has anointed my body beforehand for burial. [9] And truly, I say to you, wherever the Gospel is proclaimed in the whole world, what she has done will be told in memory of her."

There are ten reflections on this event that helps us to learn precious lessons:

i. A woman whose name is not mentioned, because mentioning the name is not significant - this is God's way
ii. The woman brings very costly anointment, breaks the flask and pours it out
iii. People get indignant - this is the human way
iv. People question - this is the human way
v. People argue about the anointment's worth - this is the human way
vi. People's concern for the poor - a human way
vii. God looks at what the woman did - God's way
viii. God's point about the poor - God's way
ix. The woman anointed for a purpose - God's way
x. The instance would be told to all of humanity

Exaltation Comes from God

Today every believer bows his knee before the Lord Jesus but one day every human being will bow, confessing Jesus. That will be the day of condemnation for them. It will be too late.

3. God's way is His honor

Phil. 2:11 and every tongue confess that Jesus Christ is Lord, to the glory of God the Father.

God exalts a person but the glory goes to God. He cannot give His glory to anyone.

Acts 12:21-23 [21] On an appointed day Herod put on his royal robes, took his seat upon the throne, and delivered an oration to them. [22] And the people were shouting, "The voice of a god, and not of a man!" [23] Immediately an angel of the Lord struck him down, because he did not give God the glory, and he was eaten by worms and breathed his last.

What does the word "confess" mean? Let us look at the meaning from the Greek word: ἐξομολογέω. It means to agree, consent, confess, admit, acknowledge, praise or thank.

Please note the name; Jesus means salvation, Christ means the Anointed and in Hebrew it means Messiah. The doctrine of the name of Jesus Christ is important for repentance and salvation as we see in the following verses:

Romans 10:9-11 [9] because, if you confess with your mouth that Jesus is Lord and believe in your heart that God raised him from the dead, you will be saved. [10] For with the heart one believes and is justified, and with the mouth one confesses and is saved.

[11] For the Scripture says, "Everyone who believes in him will not be put to shame."

Acts 2:36 Let all the house of Israel therefore know for certain that God has made him both Lord and Christ, this Jesus whom you crucified."

Acts 2:38 And Peter said to them, "Repent and be baptized every one of you in the name of Jesus Christ for the forgiveness of your sins, and you will receive the gift of the Holy Spirit.

Other such references include Acts 3:6; 4:10; 8:12; 9:34; 10:36 and 28:31.

What does it mean to confess in your daily life?

- In your daily prayers, acknowledge Him as the Lord Jesus Christ.
- In your home in your family prayers, pray with meaning and understanding; don't sleep while praying.
- In your witnessing life, live out Acts 2:38: "And Peter said to them, 'Repent and be baptized every one of you in the name of Jesus Christ for the forgiveness of your sins, and you will receive the gift of the Holy Spirit.' "
- Other references include: Acts 4:10; 8:12; 9:34; 10:36; 16:18.

When you confess with your tongue:

- Your life will be transformed. You will live under His Lordship.
- Your family will live under His Lordship

Exaltation Comes from God

- You and your family will have a powerful witness to those around you.

So your tongue confesses the Lord Jesus Christ. And God gets the glory through this. That means when you don't confess, you are grieving the Holy Spirit because you are not honoring the Lord. Look again at:

> **Acts 12:21-23** [21] On an appointed day Herod put on his royal robes, took his seat upon the throne, and delivered an oration to them. [22] And the people were shouting, "The voice of a god, and not of a man!" [23] Immediately an angel of the Lord struck him down, because he did not give God the glory, and he was eaten by worms and breathed his last.

So the exhortation in 1 Corinthians 10:31 is critical: "So, whether you eat or drink, or whatever you do, do all to the glory of God."

Conclusion: Promotion in life comes from God. God is all powerful and He can bring progress in any life. He can lift somebody up from the dust and exalt him or her. But His way of doing this is through humility, true humility. So please learn this true humility from your ultimate model, the Lord Jesus Christ. God exalts you for the sake of all humanity and He will get all the glory. Are you ready for such a life?

Chapter 16

Work Out Your Own Salvation

Text: *Philippians 2:12-13* *[12] Therefore, my beloved, as you have always obeyed, so now, not only as in my presence but much more in my absence, work out your own salvation with fear and trembling, [13] for it is God who works in you, both to will and to work for his good pleasure.*

Introduction: "Work out your own salvation" sounds interesting, doesn't it? During the early years of my Christian life I learned what the two most important decisions in life are. The first one is to accept the Lord Jesus Christ as one's personal Savior and Lord and the second one is the decision about a life partner. These were engraved on my heart. This text from Philippians has to do with the first of those two decisions.

As we look around we can observe how the devil has blinded people to keep them away from the true and genuine experience of salvation. Today there are millions of people who believe that they will receive salvation by dipping in the Ganges river or making a pilgrimage to a temple in Kashmir. There are other people who believe that you need to visit Mecca in order to get salvation. The Bible teaches that salvation is "so great salvation." This salvation that the Bible speaks about is not obtained by human efforts because salvation is divine. Among the people who claim to believe the Bible there are different understandings about salvation. For example, some think they will be saved and go to heaven if they attend a church or go through the process of catechism or are christened or baptized, but none of these can save a person.

Some scholars have become proponents of the view that says the text before us, Philippians 2:12-13, isn't speaking of personal salvation which is the deliverance from sin but of the "welfare" of the whole community. This understanding came into being because the word "salvation" has different meanings. However, *there is a clear indication and belief that Paul is talking here about personal salvation that involves deliverance from sin, justification and reconciliation with the living God.*

Let us look to the text and understand what He is saying to us with the help of His Spirit. There are four keys to how a believer is to work out his or her salvation in order to live the life designed for you by God:

1. The statement is addressed to an obedient group
2. The statement admonishes them to act in genuine obedience
3. The statement appeals for an action
4. The statement shows an awareness that God is at work

Let us begin with the first aspect.

1. The statement is addressed to an obedient group

Phil. 2:12 Therefore, my beloved, as you have always obeyed

Paul's addresses the believers of Philippi as "beloved." There is a close and affectionate connection between a local congregation and their leader. This is a good model for us today. We already know that the church at Philippi had people from different backgrounds. Paul didn't distinguish between people who were from different regions. He treated everyone the same. He called everyone "beloved." This was true in many other places in Scripture too. Consider 1 Corinthians 10:14, 15:58, 2 Corinthians 7:1, 12:19 and Philippians 3:1. Paul uses the same word in the context of God's election - ἀγαπητοῖς θεοῦ, κλητοῖς ἁγίοις, which means "loved by God and called to be saints." The same word is also used in Romans 11:28: "As regards the Gospel, they are enemies of God for your sake. But as regards election, they are beloved for the sake of their forefathers."(See also Col. 3:12; 1 Thess. 1:4 and 2 Thess. 2:13.)

After this affectionate address, Paul goes on to his exhortation and commendation. The topic of his commendation is "obedience." The one whom the Philippians are obeying is debatable because of the absence of the object. I am sure, though, that if they are obeying God they are also obeying their leader on earth and if they are obeying their leader on earth who is appointed by God, they are obeying God. In Philippians 2:5-8, we have a perfect model of obedience in the Lord Jesus Christ. In the following section, verses 9-11, we have the result or outcome of His obedience. God highly exalted Him. This is the background Paul gives to now commend the obedience of the Phililppian believers. Can a Christian leader commend your obedience today? Do you have a testimony that could be spoken of like this? When you live a life of obedience, people around you know it because they can see it.

What happens when people obey God? Learn from this wonderful example. Hudson Taylor, a medical doctor, gave up his career in England and landed in China. On June 25 1865, James Hudson Taylor, at thirty three, came to the great crisis in his life. The locale was Brighton Beach on the south coast of England. There, on a quiet Sunday morning, he took a step of faith in response to a simple spiritual principle he had just discovered. He was surprised that this truth had so long eluded him. "If we are obeying the Lord, the responsibility rests with Him, not with us!" Months of struggle were over and the way ahead was clear. To obey the Scriptures and trust God to be faithful to His pledged Word was not rash. Throwing caution and tradition to the wind, Hudson Taylor formed the China Inland Mission.

Please listen to another true story. In the 1700's a little man in England, a cobbler by trade, who kept a map of the world on a wall of his workshop so that he could pray for the nations of the world, became burdened for a definite missionary outreach. When he shared his burden at a meeting of ministers, he was told by one of the senior men of God, "Young man, sit down. When God wants to convert the heathen, He will do it without your help or mine." But William Carey did not let the fire of his enthusiasm be dampened by such a response, and eventually he left the shores of England for those of India, where he engaged in pioneer missionary work, doing exploits for God." This William Carey, a cobbler, did not look at his limitation but left his country to land in India and later became a great Bible translator. He also wrote the first dictionary for Bengali speaking people. He said, "When I am gone, speak less of Dr. Carey and more of Dr. Carey's Savior."

So Paul was passionately addressing a group of obedient people. These people were always obedient. Obviously they are believers. How can disobedient people be believers? **If there is consistent disobedience, a continuous rebellion and a constant rejection of what God is telling you to do how, can you be a believer?** Please look at these verses:

Ephesians 2:1-2 And you were dead in the trespasses and sins [2] in which you once walked, following the course of this world, following the prince of the power of the air, the spirit that is now at work in the sons of disobedience

Titus 3:3-5 ³ For we ourselves were once foolish, disobedient, led astray, slaves to various passions and pleasures, passing our days in malice and envy, hated by others and hating one another. ⁴ But when the goodness and loving kindness of God our Savior appeared, ⁵ he saved us, not because of works done by us in righteousness, but according to his own mercy, by the washing of regeneration and renewal of the Holy Spirit

2. The statement admonishes them to act in genuine obedience

Phil. 2: 12 so now, not only as in my presence but much more in my *absence*

There are two parts to Paul's admonition. First, he prompts them to continue to obey. Second, he admonishes them to genuine obedience.

Let's look first at his prompting that they should continue to obey. He says that they should not be obedient children only in the presence of their leader but at all times. Look at the following verses about obedience:

- Obedience is better than a sacrifice.

1 Samuel 15:22 And Samuel said, "Has the LORD as great delight in burnt offerings and sacrifices, as in obeying the voice of the LORD? Behold, to obey is better than sacrifice, and to listen than the fat of rams.

- You are to obey your parents.

- **Colossians 3:20** Children, obey your parents in everything, for this pleases the Lord.

- You are to obey your masters.

Ephesians 6:5 Slaves, obey your earthly masters with fear and trembling, with a sincere heart, as you would Christ

- Wives are to obey their husbands.

Titus 2:5 to be self-controlled, pure, working at home, kind, and submissive to their own husbands, that the word of God may not be reviled.

Second, he admonishes them to genuine obedience. If the obedience is genuine, it will be found when nobody is watching you.

- Obedience is rewarding and that is a good motivation to obey, whether any person is watching or not.

Deuteronomy 28:2 And all these blessings shall come upon you and overtake you, if you obey the voice of the LORD your God.

Paul wants these obedient people to obey always and to do so genuinely.

3. The statement appeals for an action

Phil. 2:12 work out your own salvation with fear and trembling

Only God works to bring salvation in our hearts. One scholar, Montgomery Boice, says, "The verse does not say, 'Work for your salvation' or 'Work toward your salvation' or 'Work at your salvation.' It says, 'Work out your salvation.' And no one can work his salvation out unless God has already worked it in." (Boice, 1971)[1]

J. Dwight Pentecost says, "This 'work out' has in it the idea to 'translate.' Translate what you know into action. This is not working to attain something. Rather, because you have attained the riches of God in Christ, you are to let those riches work themselves out in your life."

How do you work out your salvation? Paul says to do so with fear and trembling. What is the meaning of this phrase "fear and trembling?" Dwight Pentecost explains,

> We noticed a great flurry of activity several blocks from home. On the sumptuous estate of one of Dallas' most prominent citizens, heavy machinery was being brought in. A long gravel driveway went curving from the street around through the trees and the shrubs to the house, which was lost behind the foliage. Bulldozers and grading equipment came in and scraped out all of that gravel. Forms were put in and concrete was poured. A new concrete driveway was completed. One could ask, "Why all this activity when there was a driveway into this estate?" we found out why. This prominent citizen was hosting President and Mrs. Johnson at dinner, and in an effort to please the President of the United States great effort was made to make his avenue of approach commodious.[2]

---

1. Montgomery Boice, James, Philippians An expostional Commentary, Baker Books, Grand Rapids, Michigan, 1971,2000, P 142.
2. Pentecost, J. Dwight, The Joy of Living, Kregel Publications, Grand Rapids, Michigan, 1973,P 89.

The two words used in Greek are: φόβου καὶ τρόμου. Lightfoot writes it is "a nervous and trembling anxiety to do right." Have you ever thought of that in regard to "fear and trembling?" There are many today who do not have any fear of God at all! It is so dangerous! We need to remind ourselves again and again about what Paul said here. The same words are used in 2 Corinthians 7:15: "And his affection for you is even greater, as he remembers the obedience of you all, how you received him with fear and trembling."There is a wide range of Greek word groups for phobos. In English, these words are fear, which could refer to alarm or fright or dismay at the time of danger and it could also mean reverence or respect in the presence of humans or God.

When there is no fear of God, people fall into all kinds of sins against God. Be careful; this is a warning! Think of Eli's sons and how they offered sacrifices at the altar. Think of the sons of Aaron, the priests who were killed because of the strange actions at the altar.

4. The statement shows an awareness that God is at work

Phil. 2:13for it is God who works in you, both to will and to work for his good pleasure.

Now the last aspect of what it means to work out your salvation is to know that it is not that you are working alone but that you are working alongside God! In the first chapter of Philippians, Paul talked about God's work in the life of the saints at Philippi. It was God who began the good work, he said. It was made clear that it was God who was working. This is supported by many other references that salvation is brought about only by God and it is His work. It is a fact that God works in you. He works in you through His Word and in response to your prayers to Him.

Let me illustrate this from the life of Abraham Lincoln. Abraham Lincoln was known as a man who read his Bible.

Joseph R. Sizoo, one – time pastor of the New York Avenue Presbyterian Church in Washington which Abraham Lincoln often attended, says he will never forget the day he held in his hands for the first time the Bible from which Lincoln's mother had read to him as a child. She had taught him to commit to memory many of its passages. It was the only possession Lincoln carried from Pigeon Creek to the Sangamon River. And book in my hand, I wondered where it would fall open. It opened to a page which was thumb marked and which he must have read many times. It was the thirty-seventh Psalm. "Fret not thyself because of evildoers ... Rest in the Lord, and wait patiently for him" (Ps 37:1, 7).

God works and wills for His good pleasure. George Washington was known for his prayer for the nation.

George Washington found rest and relief in prayer during the trying times he and his soldiers passed through at Valley Forge. With all the cares and anxieties of that time upon him, he used to have recourse to prayer. One day a farmer approaching the camp heard an earnest voice. On coming nearer, he saw George Washington on his knees, his cheeks wet with tears, praying to God. The farmer returned home and said to his wife, "George Washington will succeed! George Washington will succeed! The Americans will secure their independence!"

There is another man who is a model of a man of the Word and prayer. He is from India (prior to partision of

Pakistan). Bro. Bakth Singh has two engineering degrees. He gave up all the glamour of the western world and was willing to wander in the city of Mumbai in order to preach the Gospel. He had no house or shelter for 10 years. He never ever had a house of his own until he passed into glory. But remember this, he planted several hundred churches in India and abroad that are now strong and healthy churches. Obedience is always rewarding whether the reward comes during your lifetime or after you are gone away. Bro. Bakth Singh knew what it meant to read his Bible several hours a day and spend many hours in prayer. During the early part of his life, he read the Bible over 100 times!

Conclusion: Salvation is the most important issue in your life. Make sure that you have a clear understanding from the Bible about what salvation really is. Work out your salvation with fear and trembling. Know for sure that it is God who is working in your life. Are you allowing Him to work? If you delay in responding to His work, you are disobeying Him. If you don't allow Him to work in your life, you are disobeying and quenching the Spirit of God.

Chapter 17

Life Designed by God for His Child

Text: ***Philippians 2:14-16*** *[14] **Do all things without grumbling or questioning,** [15] **that you may be blameless and innocent, children of God without blemish in the midst of a crooked and twisted generation, among whom you shine as lights in the world,** [16] **holding fast to the word of life, so that in the day of Christ I may be proud that I did not run in vain or labor in vain.***

Introduction: In our previous chapter we observed four keys to "working out your own salvation." We are not told to work toward our own salvation but that it is God who works in our lives for His will and good pleasure. This truth came just after Paul's exhortation on humility and the result of humility in the life of Christ, which was His exaltation. This is a sure motivation for every believer to live a blameless and innocent life. There is no excuse because of the example we have in the Lord Jesus Christ. Who is your model in life? Now God who is at work in our lives has designed a life for us to live on this earth. This present text commands us to "Do all things without grumbling and questioning" and to "live without blemish."

You are living in the midst of a crooked and twisted generation. This means you are in the midst of crooked and twisted ideologies, philosophies and lifestyles. All of these have a great influence on movies, TV shows, radio programs and such. As you watch them, take a keen interest in them and indulge in them, you are perverted and defiled. Daniel in the Old Testament lived in such circumstances but look at what God says in Daniel 1:8: "But Daniel resolved that he would not defile himself with the king's food, or with the wine that he drank. Therefore he asked the chief of the eunuchs to allow him not to defile himself."

Moses lived among a difficult people as well.

> **Deuteronomy 9:12-17** [12] Then the LORD said to me, 'Arise, go down quickly from here, for your people whom you have brought from Egypt have **acted corruptly**. They have **turned aside quickly** out of the way that I commanded them; they have **made themselves a metal image**.' [13] "Furthermore, the LORD said to me, 'I have seen this people, and behold, it is a **stubborn people**. [14] Let me alone, that I may **destroy them** and blot out their name from under heaven. And I will make of you a nation mightier and greater than they.' [15] So I turned and came down from the mountain, and the mountain was burning with fire. And the two tablets of the covenant were in my two hands. [16] And I looked, and behold, **you had sinned** against the LORD your God. You had made yourselves a **golden calf**. You had turned aside quickly from the way that the LORD had commanded you. [17] So I took hold of the two tablets and threw them out of my two hands and broke them before your eyes.

The bolded words in the above passage show the kind of people with whom Moses lived.

I will never forget my childhood days when I had a movie star as my hero. I even made my hairstyle to look like his. One morning I got ready for school and combed my hair to look like the celebrity's hair. My sisters saw this and complained it to my Dad. Lo and behold! My dad, who was a disciplinarian, approached me and gave me a good bashing and changed my hairstyle completely. He said, "Who is your model?" It is good to have some discipline at home. I never appreciated my dad's attitude at that time but now I certainly do though I don't recommend to parents such beating.

How are we commanded to live in this passage? There are three important characteristics of this life found in the text. It is to be a:

1. Life without grumbling or questioning
2. Life without blemish
3. Life with the Word of life

Is it possible to live a life that is blameless and innocent? If so, how is it possible? The only way it is possible is through the death and resurrection of the Lord Jesus Christ. The power of the resurrection is sufficient for us to lead a new life that is blameless and innocent. Are you living that life? What is this life we are talking about?

1. Life without grumbling or questioning

Phil. 2:14-15 [14] Do all things without grumbling or questioning,[15] that you may be blameless and innocent

First, we are commanded to "do all things." "Do" is Πάντα. It is an adjective indefinite accusative neuter plural no degree, πᾶς, πᾶσα, πᾶν gen. παντός, πάσης, παντός without the article each, every (pl. all), every kind of, all, full, absolute or greatest.

This means you are to do "all" or "each" or "every thing." This refers not only to good circumstances but to difficult circumstances too and with difficult tasks that you encounter. Everything is to be done without grumbling or questioning. That is the directive from God. It is not just "do all things" but "do all things without grumbling and questioning." The word for grumbling is γογγυσμῶν. It is a noun genitive masculine plural common and means complaining, whispering or quarreling. The pronunciation of this Greek word sounds like muttering.

The picture of the Israelites is a warning for every believer. The Lord brought them out from bondage and did great miracles in their lives. But the Israelites grumbled and God heard it. **1 Corinthians 10:10:** "nor grumble, as some of them did and were destroyed by the Destroyer."

The word for questioning is διαλογισμῶν. It is a noun genitive masculine plural common and means opinion, motive (κριταὶ δ. πονηρῶν perhaps persons who make judgments based on evil motives Jas 2:4), reasoning, doubt, question, argument or dispute.

This means you should not have disputes or arguments that lead to an unhealthy atmosphere. This situation leads to loss of fellowship with one another and ultimately to hatred for one another. Anger takes hold of you and can lead to all kinds of sinful activities. This is not permissible in the life that is designed for you by God.

Secondly, this command has definitive results in one's life. The Lord directs you not to grumble or question because if you obey these commands, you will able to be blameless and innocent. To be "blameless" is to be a testimony to those around you. Innocence is a factor of your internal life. This covers every aspect of your complete life - life that is internal and is also displayed externally. You have a testimony that is both internal and external. If you do not grumble or question, you will be blameless and innocent. This is the life designed by God for you.

2. Life without blemish

Phil. 2:15 children of God without blemish in the midst of a crooked and twisted generation, among whom you shine as lights in the world

What is to be the condition of the children of God? The children of God are to live a life without blemish. The word in Philippians 2:15 ἄμωμα means faultless or without blemish. How does one become a child of God? John 1:12 tells us, "But to all who did receive him, who believed in his name, he gave the right to become children of God."

So a child of God is to be without blemish. Consider John's words in the following passage:

1 John 3:1-6 See what kind of love the Father has given to us, that we should be called children of God; and so we are. The reason why the world does not know us is that it did not know him. ² Beloved, we are God's children now, and what we will be has not yet appeared; but we know that when he appears we shall be like him, because we shall see him as he is. ³ And everyone who thus hopes in him purifies himself as he is pure. ⁴ Everyone who makes a practice of sinning also practices lawlessness; sin is lawlessness. ⁵ You know that he appeared to take away sins, and in him there is no sin. [6] No one who abides in him keeps on sinning; no one who keeps on sinning has either seen him or known him.

But being a child of God is not without challenges in this life. What is one of those challenges? You must live among a crooked and twisted generation. In the first sermon that Peter preached he referred to the crooked generation. We read in Acts 2:40; "And with many other words he bore witness and continued to exhort them, saying, 'Save yourselves from this crooked generation.' "

Moses used the same words when he spoke of the Israelites in the Old Testament.
Deuteronomy 32:5: "They have dealt corruptly with him; they are no longer his children because they are blemished; they are a crooked and twisted generation."

    3.   Life with the Word of life

Phil. 2:16 holding fast to the word of life, so that in the day of Christ I may be proud that I did not run in vain or labor in vain.

We'll look at three aspects of life with the Word of Life.

    i) Hold fast

A more accurate translation of the verb would be "holding forth." This means giving out the Word of life to others, passing it on. How do you hold fast or hold forth God's Word?

- Regularly meditate on His Word
- Revere His Word
- Retain His Word

- Relate His Word to all of life – let the Word of life naturally flow out from you

This Word of life guides you (Isa. 30:21), guards you (Ps 119:11) and governs you (Ps 119:105).

ii) Heavenward look

The verse points us to the day the Lord appears, the day final events begin to happen. It is the day when we will appear before Christ (refer back to Phil. 1:6 on the day of Christ).

iii) Heed the instruction to be fruitful

Galatians 2:2I went up because of a revelation and set before them though privately before those who seemed influential the Gospel that I proclaim among the Gentiles, in order to make sure I was not running or had not run in vain.

Paul did not waste his time. He did not waste his resources. He went through life with a purpose. That is our model for us today. Do not do anything in life in vain. How is this possible? It is possible by knowing God's will for your life. Paul's motto was to know God's will and do it. "And I said, 'What shall I do, Lord?' And the Lord said to me' " (Acts 22:10).

Conclusion: As you look heavenward during the time you live in the midst of crooked and twisted generation on earth, you are commanded to live the life that is designed for you by God. He commands you not to murmur or question so that you will be blameless and innocent. Live so as to be a child of God without blemish, doing nothing in vain. You want to be a good steward because you will stand before Him on the day of Christ.

Chapter 18

Make Your Sacrifice with Joy

Text: *Philippians 2:17-18* *¹⁷ Even if I am to be poured out as a drink offering upon the sacrificial offering of your faith, I am glad and rejoice with you all. ¹⁸ Likewise you also should be glad and rejoice with me.*

Introduction: This may well be the most difficult topic to deal we've faced thus far in Philippians. Make your sacrifice with joy. This applies to every believer. Are you ready, if God is speaking to you on the subject of sacrifice?

Both the Old Testament and the New Testament teach on sacrifices. Paul uses the same word for sacrifice here that he used in Romans 12:1. The word θυσία means an act of offering or sacrifice. He used the same word in Ephesians 5:2 when he said, "As Christ loved us and gave himself up for us, a fragrant offering and sacrifice to God." The word for this in Hebrew is מִנְחָה and means gift, present, tribute or offering of any kind whether of grain or animals.

Paul's theology is very clear and strong that the believer is identified with the Lord Jesus Christ. He doesn't compromise on that. Every believer, when he or she accepts the Lord Jesus Christ as his or her personal Savior and Lord, is immersed into Christ. But Paul's teaching cannot be practiced apart from a sacrificial life. Romans 6 speaks of the same truth. Paul says in Galatians 2:20: "I have been crucified with Christ. It is no longer

I who live, but Christ who lives in me. And the life I now live in the flesh I live by faith in the Son of God, who loved me and gave himself for me." This is where the teachings of the Bible are different from the "health, wealth and prosperity Gospel" because the life of discipleship demands sacrifice. I don't see any discipleship in the health, wealth and prosperity Gospel.

What does sacrifice mean to you today? In the religions of the world, the meaning of baptism has no value if you do not know by personal experience what it means to put yourself on the altar of God. The desires of the flesh, the motives of the flesh, the crooked life that you practiced, the cleverness of the world that you adopted is all crushed into pieces. You no longer want to employ these tactics in your life. You want to trust the Lord each day of your life, abide with Him each moment and walk with Him for all of your life. Do you know this kind of life by experience? The Bible says that a life like this is possible. God made every provision for us to have this life.

> **Ephesians 4:11-14** [11] And he gave the apostles, the prophets, the evangelists, the pastors and teachers, [12] to equip the saints for the work of ministry, for building up the body of Christ, [13] until we all attain to the unity of the faith and of the knowledge of the Son of God, to mature manhood, to the measure of the stature of the fullness of Christ, [14] so that we may no longer be children, tossed to and fro by the waves and carried about by every wind of doctrine, by human cunning, by craftiness in deceitful schemes.
>
> **Colossians 1:28-29** [28] Him we proclaim, warning everyone and teaching everyone with all wisdom, that we may present everyone mature in Christ. [29] For this I

toil, struggling with all his energy that he powerfully works within me.

Let us look at the text prayerfully and respond positively in order to live it practically. There are two sides to the coin of making a sacrifice with joy.

1. A meaningful offering accompanies joy
2. A mutual participation in the sacrifice accompanies joy

Do you rejoice when you make sacrifices? The text teaches us to rejoice in our sacrifices.

1. A meaningful offering accompanies joy

Phil. 2:17 Even if I am to be poured out as a drink offering upon the sacrificial offering of your faith, I am glad and rejoice with you all.

Paul speaks of being a libation that is poured out as a liquid. He looks at the Philippian believers as priests, doing the service of God. He says that you are to pour out your life as a drink offering with joy and that this priestly life brings joy. There are commentators who say that Paul is talking about his death. In the English Standard Version translation, the conjunction "but" is not translated but the New American Standard Bible translation does translate this word. In the original text, αλλα is a coordinating conjunction. There is an emphasis added in the meaning, "But even if I am to be poured out." Scholar Lightfoot interprets this as "If I am required to pour out my life-blood as a libation over the sacrificial offering of your faith."[1] This interpretation is very close to the Urdu

---

1. Lightfoot, J.B., St. Paul's Epistle to the Philippians, Zondervan Publishing House, Grand Rapids, Michigan, first printing 1953, P 118.

translation of the verse. It says, "Aur agar mujhe tumhare iman ki qurbani aur khidmat ke sath apna khun bhi bahana pare…" In the original text there is no mention of "blood" but it simply says σπενδομαι meaning "I pour out as a drink offering." In ancient times, an animal was sacrificed and wine was poured in front of or on the top of the altar. Paul used the same word when he talked about his own death in 2 Timothy 4:6: "For I am already being poured out as a drink offering, and the time of my departure has come."

If the words are to be interpreted literally we would read Philippians 2:17 Ἀλλὰ εἰ καὶ As "but if I." The text here in Greek points to the extremity of the condition. In verse 16, Paul talks about his labors. Here is verse 17, he says that even if death happens, he is determined to go all the way with joy. The translation of σπενδομαι is "being poured out." The verb here is in the present tense. This suggests that he is talking about his present situation and not his future death. In the introduction we saw that Paul talked about sacrificial living in the book of Romans. Please read again:

> **Romans 6:4-11** [4] We were buried therefore with him by baptism into death, in order that, just as Christ was raised from the dead by the glory of the Father, we too might walk in newness of life. [5] For if we have been united with him in a death like his, we shall certainly be united with him in a resurrection like his. [6] We know that our old self was crucified with him in order that the body of sin might be brought to nothing, so that we would no longer be enslaved to sin. [7] For one who has died has been set free from sin. [8] Now if we have died with Christ, we believe that we will also live with him. [9] We know that Christ being raised from the dead will never die again; death no longer has dominion over him.

¹⁰ For the death he died he died to sin, once for all, but the life he lives he lives to God. ¹¹ So you also must consider yourselves dead to sin and alive to God in Christ Jesus.

It is in the present situation that we are exhorted to live by pouring out our lives. This is a metaphorical use. If we look at the context, it helps us to know that Paul was not talking about his martyrdom. "And I trust in the Lord that shortly I myself will come also" (Phil. 2:24).

So Paul was pouring out his life as a drink offering. This is a sacrificial life and it is not possible without the operation of the cross in our lives. This pouring out can be made today in our lives in many practical ways.

- You pour out your life in building others. This means you are investing time and energy into the lives of others. This results in "kingdom building."
- You pour out your life in serving God. You give your time and money and keep doing His will. This results in glorifying God.

Paul says that he is being poured out as a drink offering as the sacrificial offering of faith. This priestly life brings joy. The Greek word in Philippians 2:17 λειτουργία means "service, ministry, worship, offering or sacrifice." According to a commentary on the Greek text, λειτουγια, "its cognate verb λειτουργεω (serve) had to do with all kinds of public service in the Greek world. In LXX both words were used almost exclusively for the service of priests and Levites in the temple (both terms appear particularly in those sections which describe priestly functions and ritual, e.g Exod. 28-39; and Ezek. 40-46."[2]

Are the Philippian believers priests? Please look at 1 Peter 2:9: "But you are a chosen race, a royal priesthood, a holy nation, a people for his own possession, that you may proclaim the excellencies of him who called you out of darkness into his marvelous light."

As priests of the Lord, we:

- Offer praises to Him
- Serve Him
- Pray on behalf of others

The Philippian believers were doing the service of the Lord. They were supporting Paul in matters of finance.

Philippians 4:10-20 [10] I rejoiced in the Lord greatly that now at length you have revived your concern for me. You were indeed concerned for me, but you had no opportunity. [11] Not that I am speaking of being in need, for I have learned in whatever situation I am to be content. [12] I know how to be brought low, and I know how to abound. In any and every circumstance, I have learned the secret of facing plenty and hunger, abundance and need. [13] I can do all things through him who strengthens me. [14] Yet it was kind of you to share my trouble. [15] And you Philippians yourselves know that in the beginning of the Gospel, when I left Macedonia, no church entered into partnership with me

---

2. O'Brien, Peter. T., The Epistle to the Philippians, A commentary on the Greek Text, William B. Eerdmans publishing company, Grand Rapids, Michigan, 1991, P 308.

Make Your Sacrifice with Joy

in giving and receiving, except you only. ¹⁶ Even in Thessalonica you sent me help for my needs once and again. ¹⁷ Not that I seek the gift, but I seek the fruit that increases to your credit.¹¹⁸ I have received full payment, and more. I am well supplied, having received from Epaphroditus the gifts you sent, a fragrant offering, a sacrifice acceptable and pleasing to God. ¹⁹ And my God will supply every need of yours according to his riches in glory in Christ Jesus. ²⁰ To our God and Father be glory forever and ever. Amen. They are involved in the partnership in the Gospel.

Philippians 1:7 It is right for me to feel this way about you all, because I hold you in my heart, for you are all partakers with me of grace, both in my imprisonment and in the defense and confirmation of the Gospel. They are open to God's servants in their midst.

Philippians 2:28-30 ²⁸ I am the more eager to send him, therefore, that you may rejoice at seeing him again, and that I may be less anxious. ²⁹ So receive him in the Lord with all joy, and honor such men, ³⁰ for he nearly died for the work of Christ, risking his life to complete what was lacking in your service to me.

    The sacrificial services of the believers at Philippi were done by faith. This is an important quality in the spiritual lives of the believers. Paul was very observant and he noticed the same quality in the lives of the Thessalonians. Please see 1 Thessalonians 1:3: "remembering before our God and Father your work of faith and labor of love and steadfastness of hope in our Lord Jesus Christ."

When you live by faith and work by faith, you are honoring the Lord. Now, Paul is glad and rejoices over these facts, the facts that refer to a meaningful offering. Please ponder those facts to observe how "sacrificial" his activities are and then let them penetrate your heart so that you can know how you, too, can rejoice in the midst of sacrifices in life.

2. A mutual participation in the sacrifice accompanies joy

Phil. 2:18 Likewise you also should be glad and rejoice with me.

Please remember that the content and the context is that of an offering to God and sacrificial service. Paul is exhorting the believers to be glad and rejoice. It was not wealth and prosperity. It was not even good health. It was a life that was being poured out. Paul was confident of his message and was living it himself. He wrote to the Philippian believers from prison. There are sixteen times that the word "rejoice" or its cognates occur in the epistle. As a leader, Paul was himself a model of sacrificial living. What does it mean to you to "rejoice?" Is it some kind of happiness? Has it to do with moods of the mind? What does it mean to rejoice?

Rejoicing is a discipline of the heart no matter what moods would mobilize you or what your circumstances are. It is a discipline of the heart to know who God is as revealed in the Bible and be willing to submit to Him at all times. To rejoice is to have joy that is not circumstantially bound but spiritually produced. This means that you are rejoicing when things are going wrong. It means you are rejoicing in the Lord when things are going well and not in "the things." This means you are not overtaken by the good things that surround you but by the Giver Himself.

Rejoicing is a missing jewel in the lives of believers today! Please look at the following references:

Romans 5:10-11 [10] For if while we were enemies we were reconciled to God by the death of his Son, much more, now that we are reconciled, shall we be saved by his life. [11] More than that, we also rejoice in God through our Lord Jesus Christ, through whom we have now received reconciliation.

Philemon 1:7 For I have derived much joy and comfort from your love, my brother, because the hearts of the saints have been refreshed through you.

1 Kings 1:40 And all the people went up after him, playing on pipes, and rejoicing with great joy, so that the earth was split by their noise.

Nehemiah 12:43 And they offered great sacrifices that day and rejoiced, for God had made them rejoice with great joy; the women and children also rejoiced. And the joy of Jerusalem was heard far away.

There is a mutual understanding and experience between Paul and the believers. Rejoicing over this mutual experience becomes possible because of the obvious connection between them. Paul exhorts them to rejoice with him.

"Likewise" and "rejoice with me" point to the fact that they are rejoicing together for the same reason. The leader and the congregation are on the same page in their understanding. Paul exhorts them to make sacrifices and let rejoicing accompany the sacrifices.

Conclusion: Make sacrifices in your life with joy, sacrifices that come out of your love for God and are made joyfully. The discipline for each day should be to:

- Get up early to wait on Him,
- Shut off the TV and radio when it is diverting you from His path
- Discipline yourself to talk to others about the Lord Jesus Christ
- Give generously to the Lord
- Love others
- Esteem others more than yourself
- Discipline yourself to shut your mouth when you are tempted to retaliate

Chapter 19

People with a Profound Testimony, Part One

Text: *Philippians 2:19-24* *¹⁹ I hope in the Lord Jesus to send Timothy to you soon, so that I too may be cheered by news of you. ²⁰ For I have no one like him, who will be genuinely concerned for your welfare. ²¹ They all seek their own interests, not those of Jesus Christ. ²² But you know Timothy's proven worth, how as a son with a father he has served with me in the Gospel. ²³ I hope therefore to send him just as soon as I see how it will go with me, ²⁴ and I trust in the Lord that shortly I myself will come also.*

Introduction: The Apostle Paul points out two people in verses 19-30 of chapter two. They are Timothy and Ephaproditus. Timothy's name is already mentioned in Philippians 1:1 but in verses 19-24 there is something special mentioned about him. The mention of these two names might appear to be out of context and some commentators have had problems understanding these verses but we know that this is the inspired Word and, therefore, there is something special for us in this text.

Who are the people who have a profound testimony? Are they the influential elite from the society? Are they the ones who give the most, financially, to the church? Who are they? In the text we see the clear testimonies of Timothy and Ephaproditus whose lives had a profound impact on the local church. In Philippians 2:19-24, Paul tells us of Timothy's testimony. Let's consider what Paul saw in Timothy and ponder our own spiritual lives in light of this text.

There are incidents taking place around us that are a good reminder and motivation for us to live for the present and the future. As I was preparing this message, I was shocked to hear of the deaths of several individuals. While driving home one night this week, I was shocked when I heard on the radio of the death of Christopher Laurie, son of preacher and evangelist Greg Laurie. I then received a prayer request via email from a friend saying his cousin's only son, only 22 years old, had died in an accident at a firing range. These incidents are realities in life. One day death will come to us all but until then, we are accountable for how we live on this earth! You may have heard the saying, "If you want to plant for a lifetime, plant a tree but if you want to plant for eternity plant a church."When the Lord Jesus Christ comes the second time, the church will go into eternity with Him. When you serve the church you are doing something that will remain for eternity. But remember there are always temporal things in this world that will come along in this life to distract us.

The following three characteristics are vital if you are to have a profound testimony, if you are to be a blessing to the local church:

1. Purposeful mission
2. Powerful testimony
3. Proven as trustworthy

As you learn about Timothy's testimony, may it be for the purpose that your own life will have a profound testimony.

People with a Profound Testimony, Part One

1. Purposeful mission

Phil. 2:19 I hope in the Lord Jesus to send Timothy to you soon, so that I too may be cheered by news of you.

In order to have a profound testimony you must be in divine hands. That means your relationship with God affects the way you move from place to place. Then you will be a source of cheer in the lives of others.

While the Lord Jesus was on earth, He moved from place to place with a purposeful mission. He was available in the night for Nicodemus. He was there at the well, just to meet the needs of one Samaritan woman who had five husbands. He was available to the sick person at Bethesda, a man who had been ill for 38 years. This shows us that our life on earth also needs to be purposeful and lived with a mission. We cannot live without direction or aim. Each individual has a mission to fulfill.

God is looking for those who are actively involved in His service. Perhaps God will revolutionize some lives through His Word to repent and get involved in His work. So please open your heart to receive what God has to say from His Word. You are not to be like a worldly man who sees his plans and visits as a matter of "luck." Rather, you are God's and you are taught to be in the will of God. This should include our moments, our careers, our future, and every detail of our lives. "…making the best use of the time, because the days are evil. Therefore do not be foolish, but understand what the will of the Lord is" (Eph. 5:16-17). "…yet you do not know what tomorrow will bring. What is your life? For you are a mist that appears for a little time and then vanishes. Instead you ought to say, 'If the Lord wills, we will live and do this or that' " (Jas. 4:14-15).

The word "hope" is used twice by Paul in this text. The same word is used in other places too.

- It is used in connection with our salvation.

Romans 8:24-25 [24] For in this hope we were saved. Now hope that is seen is not hope. For who hopes for what he sees? [25] But if we hope for what we do not see, we wait for it with patience.

- It is used for divine love that should be in every believer.

1 Corinthians 13:7 Love bears all things, believes all things, hopes all things, endures all things.

- It is also used with regards to faith.

Hebrews 11:1 Now faith is the assurance of things hoped for, the conviction of things not seen.

The "hope" that Paul is talking about is an expectation that finds its basis in the divine realm, meaning you cannot humanly make it happen. As a believer, it is important to know that we are in the divine hands of God and that it is God who works in His sovereignty, justice and love to accomplish the things for which we hope.

So Paul hopes to send Timothy. And he wants to send Timothy soon. The word for "soon" in Greek is ταχέω and is used also in Luke 14:21 where we have the story of people being called to a banquet. The invited people made various excuses so the order was given to the servant to go "quickly" and gather in other people, the lame, the blind and such.

Please remember where Paul was when he planned to send Timothy. Paul was a good planner and every leader needs to be such a planner. Paul was in prison but his joy came from the news of the Philippian church because Paul was so deeply connected with them.

Does the news of a local church cheer you up? Are you connected with your local church? What are the things of the local church that make you either sad or happy? Though the Apostle Paul experienced all kinds of hardships he said that the weight of the local church was heavy on him.

2 Corinthians 11:28-30 [28] And, apart from other things, there is the daily pressure on me of my anxiety for all the churches. [29] Who is weak, and I am not weak? Who is made to fall, and I am not indignant? [30] If I must boast, I will boast of the things that show my weakness.

That is a good model for us. Timothy followed Paul's example in having a Christ-like concern for others.

2. Powerful testimony

Phil. 1:20-21 For I have no one like him, who will be genuinely concerned for your welfare [21] They all seek their own interests, not those of Jesus Christ.

Please don't misunderstand what it means to have a powerful testimony. It does not mean a person is an energetic preacher or that he has an entertaining vocabulary or that he is an emotionally-charged teacher. The person who has a powerful testimony is the person whose life would bear a crisis, the person who would encounter difficulties with joy and would overcome temptations. Paul was a leader who was imprisoned and his people still lived triumphantly. One of them was Timothy. Paul says of Timothy, "I have no one like him, who will be genuinely concerned for your welfare and that while others are seeking their own interests and not those of Jesus Christ, that is not the case with Timothy."

Let's look more at Timothy's testimony. His concern was conspicuous, that is it was evident for all to see. He was concerned for people. Paul was very observant and noticed that Timothy's concern for the people of Philippi was genuine. This concern related to their welfare. The Greek word for "concern" indicates "being anxious" as in 1 Peter 5:7 where it says not to be anxious, meaning don't worry about anything. This is the same word, but with a good meaning.

Paul went to the extent of making a statement of comparison "I have no one like him."This may well be the result of Timothy's upbringing. "I am reminded of your sincere faith, a faith that dwelt first in your grandmother Lois and your mother Eunice and now, I am sure, dwells in you as well" (2 Tim. 1:5).

Timothy's beginnings are noteworthy.

> **Acts 16:1-3** [1] Paul came also to Derbe and to Lystra. A disciple was there, named Timothy, the son of a Jewish woman who was a believer, but his father was a Greek. [2] He was well spoken of by the brothers[1] at Lystra and Iconium. [3] Paul wanted Timothy to accompany him, and he took him and circumcised him because of the Jews who were in those places, for they all knew that his father was a Greek.

Please note that the above text speaks of the good report others made of Timothy. It was this kind of person that Paul invited to be on his team. It is very important to know what others say about you. "Let another praise you, and not your own mouth; a stranger, and not your own lips" (Prov. 27:2).

The text also talks about self interests. While there are people who only care about their own interests, the one who is related to the Lord Jesus Christ is a different kind of person. What is the interest of the Lord Jesus Christ today? Here are a couple of references to see His heart. "No, I tell you; but unless you repent, you will all likewise perish" (Luke 13:3). This means the Lord's interest is that no one should perish. Are you interested in this? If so, what are you doing about it?"But seek first the kingdom of God and his righteousness, and all these things will be added to you" (Matt. 6:33). Are you interested in yourself or interested in the things of the Lord Jesus Christ? "If then you have been raised with Christ, seek the things that are above, where Christ is, seated at the right hand of God. Set your minds on things that are above, not on things that are on earth" (Col. 3:1-2).

What will your life look like if you are seeking the things above and having the mind of Christ? You will:

- Build up His kingdom by building up lives on this earth
- Build up His kingdom by witnessing to the lost people
- Build up His kingdom by financial help
- Build up His kingdom by using your spiritual gifts
- Build up His kingdom by living every moment of your life for Him

3. Proven as trustworthy

Phil. 2: 22-24 [22] But you know Timothy's proven worth, how as a son with a father he has served with me in the Gospel. [23] I hope therefore to send him just as soon as I see how it will go with me, [24] and I trust in the Lord that shortly I myself will come also.

People with a Profound Testimony, Part One

Please notice that there is a special connection between Paul and Timothy and then between Paul, Timothy and the church at Philippi. The word for "son" is actually "child" in Greek. Timothy was available to serve alongside Paul as a child does his father. Paul was a father figure for Timothy. Timothy served in the Gospel and that is how the churches are planted.

Timothy had a proven worth. He was proven trustworthy as he served in the church and as he served for the sake of the Gospel. The Greek word for "prove" is "test." The same word is used in the verses that follow. "…for in a severe test of affliction, their abundance of joy and their extreme poverty have overflowed in a wealth of generosity on their part" (2 Cor. 8:2). When you go through severe testing in the area finances, you are to still be faithful in your giving. "For this is why I wrote, that I might test you and know whether you are obedient in everything" (2 Cor. 2:9). Paul knew his people could say that they were obedient in everything.

You must be careful that your motivation is right when you delegate work to others. Your motivation would be wrong if it was so that you could escape the responsibility of the work. But there is a right motivation to delegate work to see if the person to whom you have given the task will prove to be trustworthy.

Paul sent Timothy to the church at Philippi. Timothy was serving in the church. Paul himself went to Philippi and probably did so even after his release from prison. But in the meantime, Timothy filled the gap. Timothy was trustworthy to do the job. Paul had confidence in him. These are the kind of people we need in the church today. Are you trustworthy? Can you be entrusted with something of value? Are you a person who keeps his or her word? If you are given a responsibility, can people trust that you will get the job done?

Conclusion: Please remember that it is God's desire that we have a profound testimony. In closing, consider the testimony of Eric Liddell.

During the summer of 1924, the Olympics were hosted by the city of Paris. Liddell was a committed Christian and refused to run on Sunday (the Sabbath), with the consequence that he was forced to withdraw from the 100 metres race, his best event. The schedule had been published several months earlier, and his decision was made well before the Games began. Liddell spent the intervening months training for the 400 metres, an event in which he had previously excelled. Even so, his success in the 400m was largely unexpected. The day of the 400 metres race came, and as Liddell went to the starting blocks, an American masseur slipped a piece of paper in his hand with a quotation from 1 Samuel 2:30, "Those who honor me I will honor." Liddell ran with that piece of paper in his hand. He not only won the race, but broke the existing world record with a time of 47.6 seconds. A few days earlier Liddell had competed in the 200 metre finals, for which he received the bronze medal behind Americans Jackson Scholz and Charles Paddock, beating Harold Abrahams, who finished in sixth place. (This was the second and last race in which these two runners met.)

Chapter 20

A Profound Testimony Requires an Action - Oriented Relationship

Text: *Philippians 2:25-30* ²⁵ *But I thought it necessary to send to you Epaphroditus, my brother and fellow worker and fellow soldier, who is also your messenger and minister to my need;* ²⁶ *because he was longing for you all and was distressed because you had heard that he was sick.* ²⁷ *For indeed he was sick to the point of death, but God had mercy on him, and not on him only but also on me, so that I would not have sorrow upon sorrow.* ²⁸ *Therefore I have sent him all the more eagerly so that when you see him again you may rejoice and I may be less concerned about you.* ²⁹ *Receive him then in the Lord with all joy, and hold men like him in high regard;* ³⁰ *because he came close to death for the work of Christ, risking his life to complete what was deficient in your service to me.*

    Introduction: The tragedy in the church is many people long to be prominent but do not possess a profound testimony. Many want a lifestyle of prestige but do not possess a profound testimony. Many people desire to see themselves as pious but do not possess a profound testimony. The question is not whether you live a short life or a long life or a very long life but is your life one of a profound testimony? Those who desire a profound testimony need to know and focus on relational distinctions. Epaphroditus was known for his relational connection to God and to people. There are seven distinctives displayed in the life of Epaphroditus. These need to be true of us as well if we are to have a profound testimony.

1. Be related to God, a brother in Christ

Phil. 2:25 But I thought it necessary to send to you Epaphroditus, my brother
Please remember that unless you are related to God, you cannot be a brother to other members of the body of Christ. This affectionate word "brother" is used in this epistle more than any other epistle (Phil. 1:2, 14; 2:25; 3:1, 17; 4:1, 8, 21).

There are two aspects to understanding this distinctive. First, this kind of relationship is brought about only through God. If you are related to God, you are directly and without any reservation related to others who belong to God.

John 1:12 [12] But as many as received Him, to them He gave the right to become children of God, even to those who believe in His name

Hebrews 2:10-11 [10] For it was fitting for Him, for whom are all things, and through whom are all things, in bringing many sons to glory, to perfect the author of their salvation through sufferings. [11] For both He who sanctifies and those who are sanctified are all from one Father; for which reason He is not ashamed to call them brethren

Acts 9:17 [17] So Ananias departed and entered the house, and after laying his hands on him said, "Brother Saul, the Lord Jesus, who appeared to you on the road by which you were coming, has sent me so that you may regain your sight and be filled with the Holy Spirit."

Secondly, this kind of relationship must be applied in practical life. We are to "Be devoted to one another in brotherly love; give preference to one another in honor" (Rom.s 12:10).

The Lord brought us from various countries, backgrounds, believes and cultures and His purpose is to unite us in Him. One of the ways that is done is through bringing us together as brother and sister. Are you related to God in a personal way? If so, you are related to each other in the body of Christ which is an inseparable relation. Let no sin bring obstruction in this relationship.

2. Be related as a worker and a soldier

Phil. 2:25 and fellow worker and fellow soldier

What does it mean to be a fellow worker and soldier? Again, one must possess a profound testimony to be a fellow worker and a fellow soldier. This title "fellow worker" was also given to Apollos, Aquila and Priscilla, Aristarchus, Clement, Mark, Onesimus, Philemon, Timothy, Titus, Tychicus, etc. This is a sure indication to you and me as well as to everyone in the church that every member of the church must be a fellow worker and fellow soldier. Serve the Lord with His people. Take opportunities to serve and don't turn them down.

Secondly, the reason for such a requirement to be a worker and soldier is very obvious. If you are not a fellow worker and fellow soldier, you certainly cannot please God. To be a fellow worker, you are people-oriented and reaching out to people with love and care. This is a characteristic that should be found in every believer. If you are a soldier, you are strong in the faith and do not give up your responsibilities as a Christian when you go through temptations. The characteristic of a soldier is clearly pointed out by the Apostle Paul in **2 Timothy 2:4**: "No soldier in active service entangles himself in the affairs of everyday life, so that he may please the one who enlisted him as a soldier."

Believers often want to be like kids, not growing in maturity. If little hurts come along, they don't know how to bear them but make an issue of it and affect others around them. Their inability to bear difficulty points out the immaturity of the knowledge that they possess, that they are not mature soldiers. If you are still acting like a child and have not matured, what does that look like? Consider this humorous illustration.

Kids Speaking to God

> One little girl began her prayer like this: "Our Father, who are in heaven, hello! What be Thy name?"
> A boy who thought he knew the answer to that question, prayed: "Our Father, who art in heaven, Harold be Thy name."
> The prayer of another boy went like this: "Our Father who art in heaven, Hollywood be Thy name."
> A girl whose visiting uncle was a horse player bowed her head with a plea that God "give us this day our daily double."
> A five-year-old girl who was trying to cope with Sunday School and kindergarten at the same time came up with this charming blend of church and state: "Give us this day our daily bread, and liberty and justice for all."
> Another kindergarten child asked God to "give us this day our jelly bread."
> Then there was the little boy who prayed, "Forgive us our dentists, as we forgive our dentists."
> Another boy pleaded, "Lead us not into creation."

Or the farmer's boy who said, "Deliver us from weevils."
Another boy prayed to God to "deliver us from eagles."
And a boy climaxed his prayer like this: "For thine is the kingdom. And the power, and the glory, forever and ever, Amen and F.M.

3. Be related in ministry as messenger and minister

Phil. 2:25 who is also your messenger and minister to my need;

First, be a messenger. In order to dive a bit further into this, let me quote from William Hendricksen.
"The word messenger is literally apostle, but this term is here used in its widest sense, indicating someone who has been delegated by the church to carry out an assignment, an official representative through whom the church itself speaks and acts. In the present case the assignment was not only to bring to Paul the gift of the Philippians church but also to serve Paul in whichever way that service might be needed." (Hendriksen, 1962)[1]. This settles in our minds that we are not troubled by the word "apostle" and the fact that we can function as apostles.

Secondly, be a minister. As Hendricksen points out, the word "minister" indicates that Epaphroditus and the church of Philippi, through Epaphroditus, performed anofficial and sacred ministry that was not only for Paul, but for the Gospel. This means they rendered their service to God.[2]

4. Be related to people; have a longing for souls

---

1. Hendriksen, William New Testament Commentary, Baker Book House, Grand Rapids, Michigan, 1962. P 139,40
2. Ibid, p 40.

A Profound Testimony Requires an Action - Oriented Relationship

Phil. 2:26 because he was longing for you all

Have you ever thought of the fact that you should long for people? How is this expressed in life?

- You desire Christian maturity for others
- You understand people's difficulties in order to care for them
- You pray for others fervently and with a burden for them
- You get connected to people and develop relationships
- You call them on the phone or email them to find out why they weren't in church
- You don't hurt people with criticisms
- You offer only constructive criticism
- You make yourself a channel of blessing to others

5. Be related to people; even distressed for the concerns of others

Phil. 2:26 and was distressed because you had heard that he was sick.

This is a good example of how to be connected to a local church. Epaphroditus was from the church of Philippi and he was so well-connected that if they were troubled, he was distressed by it. That is how it should be with each other. William Hendricksen says that the word used here is the same word used for the "anguish" of the Lord Jesus Christ faced in the Garden of Gethsemane (Matt. 26:37 and Mark 14:33).[3] Another

---

3. Hendriksen, William, new Testament Commentary, Exposition of Galatians, Ephesians, Philippians, Colossians, and Philemon, Baker books, Grand Rapids, Michigan, 1968, P 141.

scholar, Gromoski, says that "it stresses mental, emotional, and spiritual anguish" Such was the kind of distress that Epaphroditus experienced. It was not superficial or insincere. That is the kind of relationship that bears profound testimony.

6. Be related with the realities of life

Phil. 2:27 For indeed he was sick to the point of death, but God had mercy on him, and not on him only but also on me, so that I would not have sorrow upon sorrow.

Epaphroditus was related to the realities of life, that is sickness and the distress that comes with it. On one occasion, I received a call from someone in my congregation. This call was different from previous ones. As soon as I asked her how she was, she said "I am in distress" and started crying. I understood the situation and gave her counsel. She stopped crying immediately and listened to me intensely and thanked me. I told her that I had used her as an illustration in introducing the message that I preached on being available to give life to others, which cheered her and encouraged her.

Hendricksen[4] mentions a list of God's people who became sick. They include: Elisha in 2 Kings 13:14, Hezekiah in 2 Kings 20:1, Lazarus in John 11:1, Dorcas in Acts 9:37, Paul in Galatians 4:13; Timothy in 1 Timothy 5:23, Trophimus in 2 Timothy 4:20.

7. Be related to others to fill in the gap; risk your life for the sake of Christ

Phil. 2:28-30 [28] Therefore I have sent him all the more eagerly so that when you see him again you may rejoice and I may be

---

4. Hendriksen

A Profound Testimony Requires an Action - Oriented Relationship

less concerned about you. [29]Receive him then in the Lord with all joy, and hold men like him in high regard; [30]because he came close to death for the work of Christ, risking his life to complete what was deficient in your service to me

First, be ready to fill the gap. Paul was in prison and couldn't go personally. Being a good administrator, he sent Epaphroditus. Secondly, receive with all joy. Paul asked the church to receive Epaphroditus with all joy. Calvin points out that "all" meant with "sincerity and abundant." Thirdly, be willing to risk your life for the sake of Christ. This is a reference to the person who takes risks in life. Is Christ worth it? Should you take risks for the sake of Gospel and the Lord Jesus Christ? Have you ever thought about this? If so, you will find yourself out of your comfort zone to take risks. Your losses on this earth for the sake of Christ will be gain in eternity.

Consider this story. It happened back in the 1950s. There was a well known radio host /comedian /songwriter in Hollywood named Stuart Hamblen who was known for his drinking, womanizing, partying, etc. One of his bigger hits at the time was "I Won't Go Hunting with you Jake, But I'll Go Chasing Women." One day, along came a young preacher holding a tent revival. Hamblen had him on his radio show, presumably to poke fun at him. In order to gather more material for his show, Hamblen showed up at one of the revival meetings. Early in the service the preacher announced, "There is one man in this audience who is a big fake." There were probably others who thought the preacher was talking about themselves, but Hamblen was convinced that he was the one the preacher was talking about. Some would call that conviction, but he would have none of it. Still the words continued to haunt him until a couple of nights later he showed up drunk at the preacher's hotel door around 2:00 a.m., demanding that the preacher pray for

A Profound Testimony Requires an Action - Oriented Relationship

him! But the preacher refused, saying, "This is between you and God and I'm not going to get in the middle of it." The preacher did invite Stuart in and they talked until about 5:00 a.m. at which point Stuart dropped to his knees and with tears, cried out to God. But that is not the end of the story. Stuart quit drinking, quit chasing women, and quit everything that was previously "fun." Soon he began to lose favor with the Hollywood crowd. He was ultimately fired by the radio station when he refused to accept a beer company as a sponsor. Hard times were upon him. He tried writing a couple of "Christian" songs but the only one that had much success was "This Old House," written for his friend Rosemary Clooney. As he continued to struggle, a long time "friend" named John took him aside and told him, "All your troubles started when you "got religion." "Was it worth it all?" Stuart answered simply, "Yes." Then his friend asked, "You liked your booze so much, don't you ever miss it?" And his answer was, "No." John then said, "I don't understand how you could give it up so easily." And Stuart's response was, "It's no big secret. All things are possible with God." To this John said, "That's a catchy phrase. You should write a song about it." And as they say, "The rest is history." The song Stuart wrote was "It Is No Secret." A portion of they lyrics say,

> *It is no secret what God can do.*
> *What He's done for others, He'll do for you.*
> *With arms wide open, He'll welcome you.*
> *It is no secret, what God can do...."*

By the way, the friend was John Wayne. And the young preacher who refused to pray for Stuart Hamblen, but talked with Hamblen and insisted that it was between Hamblen and God? That was Billy Graham.

Chapter 21

Beware for Your Safety

Text: *Philippians 3:1-6 Finally, my brothers, rejoice in the Lord. To write the same things to you is no trouble to me and is safe for you. ² Look out for the dogs, look out for the evildoers, look out for those who mutilate the flesh. ³ For we are the real circumcision, who worship by the Spirit of God¹ and glory in Christ Jesus and put no confidence in the flesh - ⁴ though I myself have reason for confidence in the flesh also. If anyone else thinks he has reason for confidence in the flesh, I have more: ⁵ circumcised on the eighth day, of the people of Israel, of the tribe of Benjamin, a Hebrew of Hebrews; as to the law, a Pharisee; ⁶ as to zeal, a persecutor of the church; as to righteousness, under the law¹ blameless.*

    Introduction: Satan will do his best to keep you from accepting the Lord Jesus Christ as your personal Savior and Lord. Once you have accepted Him as the Lord and Savior of your life, Satan will do his best to keep you distracted from the Truth. The Pharisees were religious people but they were blind to the truth. They were bound by religion and legalism that kept them from being freed from their sin. The Apostle Paul came from a strong Pharisaical background but his eyes were opened and he was saved from his sin. From that time on, he continually taught that people should beware of false doctrines that could lead them astray.

Today we are living in a time when every believer needs to be aware of those things that are a threat to our spiritual lives. We need to be ware of false teaching and false teachers. We must hold on to true spirituality. True spirituality can be defined in one statement: "Christ living in you and you living in Him, for Him, by Him and focused on Him." As previously stated, Paul was not only teaching God's Word to the early church but he was also warning them about the attacks that would come against their spiritual lives.

There are three keys to keep from going astray. They are:

1. Focus on Christ
2. Beware of spurious teaching
3. Hold on to true spirituality

People of God are always confronted with the attacks of the enemy to draw them away from God. It happened in the days of Israel in the Old Testament. It happened in the days of the early church and it is happening now. Paul was aware of the attacks of the enemy and so he warns. This is not just "information" for us but it is a strong caution and warning for us. Let's look at these keys that will keep us from going astray.

1. Focus on Christ

Phil. 3: 1 Finally, my brothers, rejoice in the Lord. To write the same things to you is no trouble to me and is safe for you.

"Finally" doesn't mean the end of the epistle but "moreover." This is a transition. The word λοιπός, means rest, remaining, from now on, henceforth, still, beyond that or in addition. So, it is better read, "Moreover not looking at other substitutes, just focus on Christ alone and in Him rejoice." This command from Paul is not just to "rejoice" but "rejoice in the Lord." The word "rejoice" occurs eight times in the epistle (twice in 1:18; 2:17, 18; 28; 3:1; and twice in 4:4).

Rejoice in nothing else but the Lord. Your achievement cannot substitute for rejoicing in the Lord. Your riches or status cannot take the place of rejoicing in the Lord. This rejoicing is not merry-making and happiness that can be bought with money. So who should rejoice? "But let all who take refuge in You rejoice" (Ps. 5:11). "I may rejoice in Your salvation. But I have trusted in Your steadfast love; my heart shall rejoice in Your salvation" (Ps. 13:5).

We are to rejoice only in the Lord. If you attempt to rejoice the way the world does, it will not be possible to rejoice in the Lord. In the Lord, rejoicing is pure, glorifying to God and satisfying to your heart.

2. Beware of spurious teaching

Phil. 3:2-6 [2] Look out for the dogs, look out for the evildoers, look out for those who mutilate the flesh. [4] though I myself have reason for confidence in the flesh also. If anyone else thinks he has reason for confidence in the flesh, I have more: [5] circumcised on the eighth day, of the people of Israel, of the tribe of Benjamin, a Hebrew of Hebrews; as to the law, a Pharisee; [6] as to zeal, a persecutor of the church; as to righteousness, under the law blameless.

Of what are you to beware?

- Dogs

Dogs were scavengers on the street. They refer to filth.

Proverbs 26:11 Like a dog that returns to his vomit is a fool who repeats his folly.

2 Peter 2:22 What the true proverb says has happened to them: "The dog returns to its own vomit, and the sow, after washing herself, returns to wallow in the mire."

Matthew 7:6 Do not give dogs what is holy, and do not throw your pearls before pigs, lest they trample them underfoot and turn to attack you.

Revelation 22:15 Outside are the dogs and sorcerers and the sexually immoral and murderers and idolaters, and everyone who loves and practices falsehood.

- Evildoers

While the Judaizers were under the impression that they were righteous workers, Paul refers to them as evildoers. True righteousness can only come from Christ based on His redemptive work on the cross.

- People who mutilate the flesh.

This is in contrast to circumcision. Circumcision is the process of "cutting around" but mutilation is "cutting off." This mutilation is forbidden in the Old Testament (1 Kings 18:28; Lev 19:28; 21:25; Deut 14:1; Isaiah 15:2; Hosea 7:14)

Circumcision is an external ordinance. The Bible teaches that the true circumcision of the heart is for cleansing from sin and not simply an external ritual (Col 2:11). Today people want to be cleansed from sin with external rituals.

However, true cleansing is done in the heart when God sees the following:

- Humility
- Repentance
- Confession
- Exercise of faith in the whole process

  • External regulations

Confidence in the flesh is an external observance. Whatever is not of faith is sin. Whatever is done in the flesh means that faith is not included in practice, expression and experience andit is not acceptable to the Lord. "But whoever has doubts is condemned if he eats, because the eating is not from faith. For whatever does not proceed from faith is sin" (Rom. 14:23).

Ever since the fall of man into sin in the Garden of Eden, man has been trying to use human ways to cover up sin. That is one way to put confidence in the flesh to experience spiritual blessings. But spiritual blessings can only come by faith. We have so many examples in the Old Testament and the New Testament that prove this point.

Paul refers to external characteristics which were true of him and which the Judaizers thought were qualifications to make one "righteous." Paul was a Hebrew and all Hebrews believe that they are the descendants of Abraham. Paul was a Pharisee which was the fundamental group and religious sect that believed and observed all external rituals to please God. So Paul says he was blameless according to the Law. But Paul was not saved through any of these means. That same message if true for everyone today, that we can trust only in God for salvation.

3. Hold on to true spirituality

Phil. 3:3 For we are the real circumcision, who worship by the Spirit of God and glory in Christ Jesus and put no confidence in the flesh

What is true spirituality? It involves true worship. The Greek word for worship means "rendering respectful service to God." The source of true spirituality is the Holy Spirit. Every believer is indwelt by the Spirit of God (Eph 1:13, John 14:16, Rom 8:16). True spirituality puts no confidence in the flesh. You cannot do anything in the flesh that is acceptable to the Lord. "For I know that nothing good dwells in me, that is, in my flesh. For I have the desire to do what is right, but not the ability to carry it out" (Rom. 7:18).

Conclusion: Know the Truth and keep knowing the Truth as this is the secret to keep you from going astray. Remember to know and practice true spirituality. Remember that true worship is rendering true spiritual service to God.

Chapter 22

A Proper Perspective of Gain and Loss Requires Self-Evaluation

Text: *Philippians 3:7-8 ⁷ But whatever gain I had, I counted as loss for the sake of Christ. ⁸ Indeed, I count everything as loss because of the surpassing worth of knowing Christ Jesus my Lord. For his sake I have suffered the loss of all things and count them as rubbish, in order that I may gain Christ.*

Introduction: Paul's testimony is outstanding and stirs the heart. To say words such as those in Philippians 3:7-8, he was either insane or intimately related to the One about Whom he spoke. Does the Bible teach on the topic of economics? That question cropped up in my mind after I read those verses. R.W. Mackey, II who contributes a chapter called, "Proposing a Biblical Approach To Economics" in John MacArthur's book, *Think Biblically!,* makes the following statement, "Although the Bible is not an economics textbook, as such, it certainly informs the economic component of a worldview. Over seven hundred passages of Scripture address the concept of wealth, either directly or indirectly." (R.W. Mackey, 2003)[1] Does the Bible speak of gain and loss? What about assets and liabilities? Paul specifically talks in Philippians about gain and loss. He evaluates loss based on Scripture. Loss is seen in light of knowing Christ.

---

1. MacArthur, John, General Editor: Think Biblically!, Crossway Books, Wheaton, Ill, 2003, P297.

A Proper Perspective of Gain and Loss Requires Self-Evaluation

Loss is traded away by self sacrifice. Paul evaluates his spiritual life and comes to a place where there is gain and profit in spite of losses. In the previous verses of chapter 3, Paul talked about his past spiritual "credentials" so to speak:

- **Circumcision**

God gave this order to Abraham and it was something to be proud of, that one kept God's command, a command given way back in the time of Abraham! Also, Paul was circumcised on the eighth day which was God's prescribed day.

- **Nation of Israel**
  Paul was from God's chosen nation of Israel.
- **Tribe of Benjamin**
  Paul was from this elite tribe of Israel.
- **A Hebrew**
  Paul was a descendent from Abraham.
- **A Pharisee**
  Paul belonged to a sect that was very strict about keeping the Law.
- **Zealous**
  Paul was zealous to the extent that he even persecuted the church and thought that he was doing God's work.
- **Observing the Law**
  Paul's self-evaluation was that he was blameless concerning the Law.

Please count these aspects of his "credentials" and you will notice that Paul listed seven credentials. This was what mattered most to him until he encountered Christ. After encountering Christ, his evaluation of his past changed. He found such lack that he abandoned those things as his

A Proper Perspective of Gain and Loss Requires Self-Evaluation

credentials. Paul traded these credentials for Christ and saw it as gain. Some of you have come from very religious backgrounds. Some perhaps have certain credentials that you think are gain. You need to examine your past experiences and past "qualifications" in the light of God's Word to know what is true gain and loss. Truly, a proper perspective of gain and loss requires self-evaluation. Please note three parts in the self-evaluation process in order to have a proper perspective of gain and loss. They are gain is loss and requires doctrinal explanation, one must lose in order to gain, which requires doctrinal enrichment and loss and gain require a doctrinally-based evaluation. We'll look at each of these in detail.

1. Gain is loss and requires doctrinal explanation

Phil. 3:7 But whatever gain I had, I counted as loss for the sake of Christ.

You may be wondering at this point if you are sitting in a university class, studying economics with all this talk about gains and losses. Well, no, you are not. We want to know from the text, though, how assets become liabilities to our spiritual life and how these liabilities are to be abandoned. Today, many people have spiritual and religious backgrounds and credentials and are under the impression that these are their assets. But they are actually liabilities.

Paul talks about his credentials, history and family line as *gain* previously and so they are assets. But these assets are of no good; they are but "dung" and are liabilities to Paul. So Paul abandons them all.

A Proper Perspective of Gain and Loss Requires Self-Evaluation

We have already noted the sevenfold facet of Paul's past. In what way is a religious background "gain" prior to coming to Christ? Here are some probable areas:

- You get outward respect from the society. The Lord Jesus Christ referred to the Pharisees and how they desired the prominent places, recognition through public worship and focus on their fasting and tithing.

- You are recognized as a religious person. The way you give and fast and act "spiritual" attracts others to give you a respected status, so you feel proud in yourself.

- Because external observations are made in the flesh, there is lot of hypocrisy and you can hide what is truly inside you. You can live a double life, a life of sin and a life of "religion." This is very appealing and pleasing to the flesh.

Consider the words of Thomas Kempis, a German ascetical writer. He said, "Many count their years since their conversion, but their lives often show little sign of improvement. If it is dreadful to die, it is perhaps more dangerous to live long. Happy is the man who keeps the hour of death always in mind, and daily prepares himself to die." That is a proper evaluation of life!

So those things that were previously gain to Paul, all those assets, are now liabilities? Liabilities to what? To Christ!

Here again is Paul's philosophy of ministry. He brings doctrine into his writings. Here is the doctrine of Christ. When you understand the doctrine of Christ and experientially know

A Proper Perspective of Gain and Loss Requires Self-Evaluation

Christ, you will want to do the same thing as Paul. The word "Christ" occurs three times in these two verses.

Here are just few reminders of what Christ has done:

- Christ became incarnate
- Christ became the intermediary
- Christ made atonement
- Christ is the LORD
- Christ is the Spirit
- Christ is the Hope
- Christ is coming back to take believers to be with Him

So why not fall at His feet? Paul acknowledged Him as his Lord, his Savior and his all in all. He submitted to Christ even as he acknowledged Him. What about you?

2. One must lose in order to gain, which requires doctrinal enrichment

Phil. 3:8 Indeed, I count everything as loss because of the surpassing worth of knowing Christ Jesus my Lord.

Here are the debits or losses: "Indeed, I count everything as loss." And here are the credits or gains: "Because of the surpassing worth of knowing Christ Jesus my Lord." All that was previously deposited in me needs to be removed or debited because it is worthless.

Let's look at the word "count." This is one of three words that occur three times in verses Philippians 3:7-8. The Greek word *hegeisthai* means to "think" or "consider" or "regard." Paul uses the word in the perfect tense *hegemai*. This

A Proper Perspective of Gain and Loss Requires Self-Evaluation

means "I count" and it implies that he had come to a final judgment only after his deliberate consideration and evaluation.

Paul is talking about counting his spiritual heritage as loss. Now "loss" is another of three words that occurs three times in these two verses. All that was previously deposited must come out or be debited. What about you? Do you have a religious heritage or credentials in your past that need to be counted as loss? Is there anything else in your life that you need to count as loss for the sake of Christ?

Recently, I was very much touched by true story. In 1903, one man started Communism with just a handful of followers. His name was Vladimir Lenin and he lived from 1870 to 1924. He overthrew the Russian government in 1917 with only 40,000 Communist Party members. His movement became the fastest growing system in the history of the world, and by the 1950s his followers controlled about 62 percent of the world's population - and brutally held on to their power. Communism triumphed largely because of the complete devotion of its followers.

One dedicated Communist, in breaking his engagement to his fiancé, wrote:
There is one thing, which I am in dead earnest about, and that is the communist cause. It is my life, my business, my religion, my hobby, my sweetheart, my wife, my mistress, and my bread and meat. I work at it in the daytime and dream of it at night. Its hold on me grows, not lessens, as time goes on; therefore, I cannot carry on a friendship, a love affair, or even a conversation without relating it to this force which both drives and guides my life. I evaluate people, looks, ideas, and actions according to how they affect the communist cause, and by their

A Proper Perspective of Gain and Loss Requires Self-Evaluation

attitude toward it. I've already been in jail because of my ideals, and if necessary, I'm ready to go before a firing squad.

While Lenin and his followers were devoted deeply to his revolution, there was another man whom God was preparing to use in His Kingdom. This man wrote more than 1,200 poems, of which 800 were published. One of them captures the devotion of his life:

Living For Jesus

>Living for Jesus a life that is true
>Striving to please Him in all that I do;
>Yielding allegiance, glad–hearted and free
>This is the pathway of blessing for me.
>
>Living for Jesus who died in my place
>Bearing on Calv'ry my sin and disgrace;
>Such love constrains me to answer His call
>Follow His leading and give Him my all.
>
>Living for Jesus wherever I am
>Doing each duty in His holy name;
>Willing to suffer affliction and loss
>Deeming each trial a part of my cross.
>
>Living for Jesus through earth's little while
>My dearest treasure, the light of His smile;
>Seeking the lost ones He died to redeem
>Bringing the weary to find rest in Him

Chorus: O Jesus, Lord and Savior, I give myself to Thee,
>For Thou in Thy atonement, didst give Thyself for me,
>I own no other Master, my heart shall be Thy throne
>My life I give, henceforth to live, O Christ, for Thee alone.

A Proper Perspective of Gain and Loss Requires Self-Evaluation

Thomas Obadiah Chisholm is the author of this poem which became a hymn. He was born in a humble log cabin in Franklin, Kentucky on July 29, 1866. Tom was weak in body, poor in health and also had very limited finances. Though he had been a door-to-door salesman, because of his health, he wasn't able to continue in his job. He spent most of his time indoors at his writing table. Writing became his first love and he penned poems such as the one above.

Please note that Paul calls Jesus Christ "my Lord." If you cannot do the things He tells you to do, don't you dare call Him your Lord. "Not everyone who says to me, "Lord, Lord," will enter the kingdom of heaven, but the one who does the will of my Father who is in heaven" (Matt. 7:21).

The young man we mentioned above who was influenced by Communism became aggressive in his commitment to communism. Thomas Chisholm whose heart was revolutionized by the Lord Jesus expressed his commitment through his writing. Paul in Philippians said that for the surpassing worth of knowing Christ, he would count everything else as loss. Paul would do this for the surpassing worth of knowing Christ. To lose in order to gain requires a doctrinal understanding and knowledge of Christ.

"Knowing" is an important word here. It doesn't mean just to have some intellectual knowledge but the Greek verb means to have a knowledge that is experiential or personal. (See also John 10:27, 17:3, 2 Cor 4:6, and 1 John 5:20.) This word corresponds with the Hebrew word that speaks of God's knowledge of His people as in Amos 3:2 and their knowledge of God as in Jeremiah 31:34, Hosea 6:3 and 8:2.

A Proper Perspective of Gain and Loss Requires Self-Evaluation

3. Loss and gain require a doctrinally-based evaluation
Phil. 3:8 For his sake I have suffered the loss of all things and count them as rubbish, in order that I may gain Christ.

Both loss and gain are used as accounting terms. Paul uses these words in reference to his spiritual transactions. The word Paul uses for loss is Σκυβαλον and it is used in the Greek world of dung, excrementor food gone bad. It is a scrap left over from a meal. The word is used only here in the New Testament. The word is used as a force to explain Paul's renunciation of his past gains. Σκυβαλα has two notions, that of filth and of worthlessness.

Γνωσισ means "knowledge" and it had a wide range of meanings during the days of Paul. It referred to a kind of mystical knowledge of or communion with the god. It was also used by Gnostic Jewish Christians and can be seen in 1 Corinthians 8:1-11; 13:2, 8; 14:6 and Galatians 4:9. It was also used to refer to the experience of martyrs. But for Paul, it would have been the concept in the Old Testament of God's knowledge of His people and His people's knowledge of Him (Exo. 33:12, 17; Amos 3:2; Jer. 31:34).

Paul has great things to say about knowing Christ, as we will see in future verses. You must have a proper knowledge of Christ and you cannot go anywhere else to find it but God's Word. You must go to Christ.

Duncan Campbell relays the following true story in *Price and Power of Revival*

Some years ago it was my privilege to share a room with that great Indian mystic, Sadhu Sundar Singh, and I remember a story he told us of a conversation that he had with a Professor of

A Proper Perspective of Gain and Loss Requires Self-Evaluation

Comparative Religions in the University of Cambridge: "Tell me," said the Professor, "what have you found in Christianity that you did not find in your old religion?" The Sadhu replied, "Professor, I found the dear Lord Jesus." "Oh, yes, I quite understand, but what particular principle or doctrine? Tell me, what new philosophy have you found in Christianity that you did not find in your old religion?" And again the Sadhu replied, "Professor, I found the dear Lord Jesus." You see, his witness was to a Person and not to a principle; to a life, and not to a philosophy - Christ was real. (Campbell)[2]

What happens when you don't have the proper knowledge of "God"? Consider the following humorous illustration.

Two Trouble Shooters

Two little boys, ages 8 and 10, are excessively mischievous. They are always getting into trouble and their parents know all about it. If any mischief occurs in their town, the two boys are probably involved.

> The boys' mother heard that a preacher in town had been successful in disciplining children, so she asked if he would speak with her boys. The preacher agreed, but he asked to see them individually. So the mother sent the 8 year old first, in the morning, with the older boy to see the preacher in the afternoon.
> The preacher, a huge man with a booming voice, sat the younger boy down and asked him sternly, "Do you know where God is, son?"

---

2. Campbell, Duncan, The price and power of Revival, The faith Mission, Edinburgh, Belfast, P 17,18.

The boy's mouth dropped open, but he had no response, sitting there wide-eyed with his mouth hanging open.

So the preacher repeated the question in an even sterner tone, "Where is God?"

Again, the boy made no attempt to answer. The preacher raised his voice even more and shook his finger in the boy's face and bellowed, "Where is God?!"

The boy screamed and bolted from the room, ran directly home and dove into his closet, slamming the door behind him.

When his older brother found him in the closet, he asked, "What happened?" The younger brother, gasping for breath, replied, "We are in BIG trouble! This time GOD is missing, and they think we did it!"

For many people, life on this earth is more precious than the life that will be hereafter. For many people, bearing the cross on this earth is too heavy so they choose not to bear it. We should remember the Lord's words, "What shall it profit a man if he gains the whole world and lose his own soul?" (Matt. 16:26). Can you say that you have suffered the loss of all things and count them as rubbish?

Conclusion: Here is the question. Are you ready to trade in your previous gains, your religious credentials? Are you willing to give up what you think is gain for the sake of Christ? What do you know about Christ that makes you reject Him? What do you know about Christ that causes you to have a lukewarm spiritual life? Do you desire to know Christ experientially in order to live for Him? Next we will look at what Philippians says about the deep knowledge of Christ that one should have.

Chapter 23

Christ has Made You His Own

Text: *Philippians 3:9-12* *[9] and be found in him, not having a righteousness of my own that comes from the law, but that which comes through faith in Christ, the righteousness from God that depends on faith- [10] that I may know him and the power of his resurrection, and may share his sufferings, becoming like him in his death, [11] that by any means possible I may attain the resurrection from the dead. [12] Not that I have already obtained this or am already perfect, but I press on to make it my own, because Christ Jesus has made me his own.*

Introduction: For the Apostle Paul, belonging to Christ was like an experience of being married to Christ. The word "know" that Paul uses has the meaning in the Old Testament of knowing the intimacy that is found between a husband and wife. Paul was 100% totally committed to Christ, sold out to Him. He was willing to give up all that he previously thought was gain. He counted it as loss and would now be sold out to Christ. This would mean yielding to the Master moment by moment. This would mean being united with Christ intimately. This might even mean being martyred. Paul's expression of belonging to Christ means that Christ has made you His own.

Do you know Christ as your personal Savior and Lord? Did you confess with your mouth that He is the Lord and do you believe in your heart that He was raised from the dead? If so, you are saved (Rom 10:9-10). Here is another question though: How far have you come since the day of your conversion? Do you know that you are united with Christ? To what extent are you united with the Lord Jesus Christ? There are seven facts which are true of the genuine believer and show you are not your own but Christ's!

1. You are the property of Christ

Phil. 3:9 and be found in him

This is a Pauline concept whereby he expresses that every believer is in Christ. This phrase occurs more than 75 times in the writings of Paul. Because you are the property of Christ, you are found in Him. Bible scholars think this refers to Paul's anticipation that his future place would be in Christ. The genuine Christian has been bought with a price. "Do you not know that you are God's temple and that God's Spirit dwells in you? (1 Cor. 3:16). "…and you are Christ's" (1 Cor. 3:23). "And such were some of you. But you were washed, you were sanctified, you were justified in the name of the Lord Jesus Christ and by the Spirit of our God" (1 Cor. 6:11). "…for you were bought with a price" (1 Cor. 6:20).

The Lord will keep His property safe until the end. Remember the truths we've seen previously in Philippians 1:6: "And I am sure of this, that he who began a good work in you will bring it to completion at the day of Jesus Christ." And 2 Timothy 4:18: "The Lord will rescue me from every evil deed and bring me safely into his heavenly kingdom. To him be the glory forever and ever. Amen."

Are you found in Him? If you have been found by Him then you are found in Him too (Luke 19:10). If you still want more assurance of this reality, read Ephesians 1 and observe the many times Paul uses the phrase, "in Him." Have you experienced that about which Paul speaks?

2. You possess Christ's righteousness

Phil. 3:9 not having a righteousness of my own that comes from the law, but that which comes through faith in Christ

Do you only have your own righteousness? Ever since the fall of man, man has tended to attempt to make up for his guilt by self efforts. Adam and Eve did that by covering themselves with leaves. God had to show His standard of holiness. He gave Moses the Law. But no man could be justified by the Law. Justification comes only by faith in Christ. "For since the law has but a shadow of the good things to come instead of the true form of these realities, it can never, by the same sacrifices that are continually offered every year, make perfect those who draw near" (Heb. 10:1).

Possessing Christ's righteousness comes at the time of rebirth. It is part of package of salvation. "If, because of one man's trespass, death reigned through that one man, much more will those who receive the abundance of grace and the free gift of righteousness reign in life through the one man Jesus Christ" (Rom. 5:17).

The Christian experience begins with faith, goes on with faith and lives forever because of faith. Without faith you can never ever live a Christian life. Forgiveness comes by faith, answers to prayers are received by faith, worship is done in faith, and we live each day by faith. You cannot make up for your guilt by any other means. You have to exercise faith in order to be reconciled with God.

Receiving the righteousness of Christ is an act of faith. You receive it by faith. You live it by faith. You enjoy it by faith. There is no place for human achievement in the true righteousness that comes from Christ. The Apostle Paul exhorted the Galatian believers in a very strong tone. "Let me ask you only this: Did you receive the Spirit by works of the law or by hearing with faith? Are you so foolish? Having begun by the Spirit, are you now being perfected by the flesh?" (Gal. 3:2-3).

3. You know the power of Christ's resurrection

Phil. 3:10 that I may know him and the power of his resurrection

The Greek word for "know" in Hebrew is yada and it is used for the intimate relationship between husband and wife. When Paul talks about knowing Christ, he is referring to knowing Christ experientially and intimately.

In the introduction to this chapter, I mentioned this word being used in the context of marriage. Please listen to the words of a man who had never been married when he wrote these words, but he speaks of marriage. C.S. Lewis, writing on the topic of Christian marriage, says, "The Christian idea of marriage is based on Christ's words that a man and wife are to be regarded as a single organism." Lewis further explained marriage with this illustration: "Just as one is stating a fact when one says that a lock and its key are one mechanism, or that a violin and a bow are one musical instrument. The inventor of the human machine was telling us that its two halves, the male and the female, were made to be combined together in pairs, not simply on the sexual level, but totally combined." (Lewis, 1980)[1]

---

1. Lewis, C.S: Mere Christianity, HarperCollins Publisher, Inc., New York, NY, 1980, P 104.

God's package of salvation includes a resurrected life. This is the divine operation of God in the spirit of man that happens at the time of conversion. I am amazed at how many things happen at the time of conversion. You receive the forgiveness of sin, reconciliation with God, the promise of the Holy Spirit, baptism into the body of Christ, you are saved, you are justified and you become the child of God. Sanctification is a process but salvation is a onetime act.

> **Romans 6:3-9** ³ Do you not know that all of us who have been baptized into Christ Jesus were baptized into his death? ⁴ We were buried therefore with him by baptism into death, in order that, just as Christ was raised from the dead by the glory of the Father, we too might walk in newness of life. ⁵ For if we have been united with him in a death like his, we shall certainly be united with him in a resurrection like his. ⁶ We know that our old self was crucified with him in order that the body of sin might be brought to nothing, so that we would no longer be enslaved to sin. ⁷ For one who has died has been set free from sin. ⁸ Now if we have died with Christ, we believe that we will also live with him. ⁹ We know that Christ being raised from the dead will never die again; death no longer has dominion over him.

4. You participate in Christ's sufferings

Phil. 3:10 and may share his sufferings

On the day of marriage, husband and wife make a vow. In the vows, we often hear the phrase, "for better or for worse." This means that the life that you begin together is really ***together*** no matter what happens for the rest of your life. You want to be with your spouse, even if it means suffering.

We are encouraged in the Scriptures to suffer for Christ.

1 Peter 4:13-14 [13] But rejoice insofar as you share Christ's sufferings, that you may also rejoice and be glad when his glory is revealed. [14] If you are insulted for the name of Christ, you are blessed, because the Spirit of glory and of God rests upon you.

5. You partake in Christ's death

Phil. 3:10 becoming like him in his death

Is the Apostle Paul insane to say such words? Wouldn't everyone prefer to enjoy life rather than death? But here he talks of becoming like Christ in His death. Have you ever said that in your prayer? Can you say that today in prayer, "Lord make me like you in your death?"

What does this kind of prayer mean today? It means:

- You will live for Him even if it means insults for His sake
- You will live the way of the cross
- You will be His servant
- You will suffer for Him
- You will be an open witness for Him

6. You have the promise of resurrection through Christ

Phil. 3:11 that by any means possible I may attain the resurrection from the dead.

When the apostle Paul says "by any means possible" does that mean he is in doubt about the resurrection? No! As John MacArthur says, "Paul is expressing humility." (MacArthur, 2001)[2]

There is going to be that glorious day of resurrection! All believers look forward to it. We are not a people without hope for the future. All the dead in Christ will rise on the day of Christ!

You are going to be raised through the power of Christ. Are you living with that hope for the future? What is that hope?

- You will have a glorious body
- You will be in heaven
- You will be with the Lord forever

7. You are to press on to be perfect because of Christ

Phil. 3:12 Not that I have already obtained this or am already perfect, but I press on to make it my own, because Christ Jesus has made me his own.

Are you on the road to perfection? Please remember the words of the Lord Jesus Christ in Matthew 5:48: "You therefore must be perfect, as your heavenly Father is perfect."

Once you become a Christian, you begin to have a hunger for God and your goal is become like Christ. We will ultimately become perfect in the areas of:
- Holiness
- Purity

---

2. MacArthur, John: The MacArthur New Testament Commentary Philippians, Moody Press, 2001, Chicago, Ill, P 240.

- Speech
- Church life
- Daily discipline of time, money and productivity

Conclusion: Christ has made you His own. Seven facts that are true of a genuine believer are:

1) You are the property of Christ
2) You possess Christ's righteousness
3) You know the power of Christ's resurrection
4) You participate in Christ's sufferings
5) You partake in Christ's death
6) You have the promise of resurrection through Christ
7) You are to press on to be perfect because of Christ.

Chapter 24

Are You Stagnant or Straining Forward?

Text: *Philippians 3:13-16* *[13] Brothers, I do not consider that I have made it my own. But one thing I do: forgetting what lies behind and straining forward to what lies ahead, [14] I press on toward the goal for the prize of the upward call of God in Christ Jesus. [15] Let those of us who are mature think this way, and if in anything you think otherwise, God will reveal that also to you. [16] Only let us hold true to what we have attained.*

Introduction: By the end of this chapter you should be able to answer the question, "Are you stagnant or straining forward?" In a competitive world, complacency is disastrous. Are we competing with each other in the Christian life? To answer this question, we need to understand that a healthy competition is not wrong. Paul talks about the race of the Christian life. That is not wrong. Complacency will make you stagnant. Stagnancy stinks. The spiritual life that is commanded by God doesn't stink but has a sweet fragrance.

In the early 1970 I came to know the Lord Jesus Christ as my personal Savior and Lord. At that time, I knew that there were areas in my life that needed to change and be transformed. I saw the Lord working in my life and changing me. One of the changes was to find a new direction for my life. My move towards a change included new relationships, a new environment, a new philosophy of life and a new ministry.

Are You Stagnant or Straining Forward?

I began attending Christian prayer meetings and home Bible studies. I began to enjoy a wonderful peace and joy in this new experience that I found through Christ. Among the thousands of Christians that I have met, one brother I met in 1972 from Chandigarh stands out in my mind. Our team stayed at his house as tenants for couple of months. His name was V.T. John, an elder in the Brethren assembly. Every morning he would bring a cup of coffee from his kitchen to give to each member of the team, about eight of us. He just recently went home to be with Lord after serving the Lord for 52 years. This brother was not stagnant in life but moving forward. He planted three churches during his 52 years of ministry. I visited two of them many years ago. Bro. V.T. John obeyed the high call of God and worked on this earth; now he has entered into his eternal rest. While on earth you have an opportunity to move forward and not be stagnant. Don't waste your years! Let us see what the apostle Paul says.

There are three keys to avoid being stagnant and to strain forward instead.

1) Overtake stagnancy by straining forward
2) Onward you go towards the goal
3) Open your heart to go forward

Let us look to the three keys that will help us to move forward.

1. Overtake stagnancy by straining forward.

Phil. 3:13 Brothers, I do not consider that I have made it my own. But one thing I do: forgetting what lies behind and straining forward to what lies ahead

Are You Stagnant or Straining Forward?

Do you know what it means to be stagnant? Let me illustrate with a statue that is in the city of Hyderabad, India. In Hyderabad there is the world's tallest statue of Buddha in the center of a famous river. When you visit that city year after year, you will see the same statue, exactly the same size and in the same place. You won't see any growth or any movement of that statue. There are many Christians who are just like that statue, showing no growth whatsoever. But the Christian life should be a life that is moving forward and not stagnant like a statue. To what should you be straining forward?

To begin with let us understand the meaning of the word "straining." Paul said he was straining forward to what lay ahead of him. According to Robert Gromacki in his commentaries on Philippians and Colossians, the word "strain" (epekteinomenos in the Greek) "denotes an athlete who runs without swerving off course and who strains his entire body to cross the finish line (Acts 20:24; 1 Cor 9: 26)." (Gromacki, 2003)[1]

Every believer needs to know that once you enter the Christian faith, you have entered the race. The race begins, goes on day after day and one day comes to an end. The end comes either when our heart stops and our human body dies or when the Lord Jesus Christ returns, which Scripture says is "imminent." "Imminence" means the event is certain to happen; only the timing of the event is uncertain.

2 Timothy 4:7-8 [7] I have fought the good fight, I have finished the race, I have kept the faith. [8] Henceforth there is laid up for me the crown of righteousness, which

---

1. Gromacki, Robert: Philippians and Colossians, Gen Editors, Mal Couch & Ed Hindson, AMG Publishers, Chattoanooga, TN, 2003, P 91.

the Lord, the righteous judge, will award to me on that Day, and not only to me but also to all who have loved his appearing.

In straining forward, you are running forward with all your strength, interest and enthusiasm. Only believers would understand this kind of life which is why Paul addresses this issue to "brothers." Yes, it is only brothers and sisters in Christ who can understand these truths. You have been brought into a new relationship through Christ.

Paul has drawn a conclusion about himself when he says "I do not consider that I have made it my own." The pronouns here are emphatic and the word "consider" means to think through. The word for consider in Greek is λογίζομαι which means, count, reckon, calculate, take into account, credit, place to one's account, consider, think, suppose, evaluate, look upon as, think on or reflect upon. This verb "consider" in the Greek world referred to "thinking according to strict logical rules." It was used as a technical term in commercial dealings for considering. The word is used 40 times in the New Testament, 34 of which are occasions when it is used by Paul. Upon careful self-examination, Paul said he had not yet attained the goal.
What causes you to be stagnant in life?

- If you won't forget the past. The past can overtake the present and overturn the future. Give the past to God, including your past defeats and victories.
- The past may be good or bad, but you need to forget it so that you'll be able to move forward.
- There is a danger of making past experiences monuments of past glory. You cannot dwell on past victories and make them idols in life. You need to move forward. The past experiences can only be an encouragement in life to move forward.

There is a future and you need to look to that.

2. Onward you go towards the goal

Phil. 3:14 I press on toward the goal for the prize of the upward call of God in Christ Jesus

"The verb press," according to Robert Gromacki, "describes vigorous, concertrated pursuit." (Gromacki, 2003)[2] There is a wonderful promise in the book of Proverbs. "When you walk, your step will not be hampered, and if you run, you will not stumble" (Prov. 4:12).

When you look at the context in which this is said you will notice that it is said to a man who is protected and guarded by the Word of God. Moving forward is:

- A planned move: Move towards the goal
- A programmed move: Move towards receiving a prize
- A purposeful move: Move for the call of God in Christ Jesus

A planned move keeps you focused. You want to reach the goal. This is how a game is played, how matches in sports are won, how Olympic medals are won and what we are encouraged to do in Scripture.

1 Corinthians 9:24 Do you not know that in a race all the runners compete, but only one receives the prize? So run that you may obtain it.

---

2. Gromacki, Robert: Philippians and Colossians, Gen Editors, Mal Couch & Ed Hindson, AMG Publishers, Chattoanooga, TN, 2003, P 91.

1 Corinthians 9:26 So I do not run aimlessly; I do not box as one beating the air.

Galatians 2:2 I went up because of a revelation and set before them (though privately before those who seemed influential) the Gospel that I proclaim among the Gentiles, in order to make sure I was not running or had not run in vain.

Hebrews 12:1 and let us run with endurance the race that is set before us

A programmed move will give you joy and happiness and motivate you to press on. Many believers lack enthusiasm and motivation in life. They want somebody to push them along every step of the way and to stand by them. These people need to grow up to be mature in the Christian life.

> **Hebrews 5:12-14** [12]For though by this time you ought to be teachers, you need someone to teach you again the basic principles of the oracles of God. You need milk, not solid food, [13] for everyone who lives on milk is unskilled in the word of righteousness, since he is a child. [14] But solid food is for the mature, for those who have their powers of discernment trained by constant practice to distinguish good from evil.

A purposeful move will keep you fervid; you will have enthusiasm. Your purpose is to receive the prize of the upward call. The prize is to possess Christ-likeness. This is the goal and it will happen one day. God will use His process of shaping your life to bring His perfect likeness in every believer. "My little children, for whom I am again in the anguish of childbirth until Christ is formed in you!" (Gal. 4:19). "Beloved, we are God's children now, and what we will be has not yet appeared; but we know that when he appears we shall be like him, because we shall see him as he is" (1 John 3:2).

That is the goal and onward you go aiming towards the goal.

3. Open your heart to go forward

Phil. 3:15-16 [15] Let those of us who are mature think this way, and if in anything you think otherwise, God will reveal that also to you. [16] Only let us hold true to what we have attained.

You need to open your heart to go forward. You cannot have any prejudice or preconceived ideas in order to receive from God and His people. The ENGLISH STANDARD VERSION translation uses the word "mature." This appears to be an accurate word in the context. The Greek word has several meanings such as complete, whole or perfect. Paul is not talking about sinless perfection because that is not possible until we get to heaven. As John MacArthur puts it, it is a "positional" perfection. (MacArthur, 2001)[3]

If people do not obey what God is saying through Paul, God uses other methods of bringing the truth to His people. For example, God uses chastening. So you need to keep your heart open for His teachings. Please remember that God is not revealing what is not already revealed in the Scriptures. In other words, there is no fresh or new revelation.

Let me illustrate this point about no new revelation with an example from a cricket match that I will never forget. It was 1986 or so and I was watching the world cup won by Pakistan. Miandad was batting. It was the last ball and Pakistan needed 5

---

3. MacArthur, John: The MacArthur New Testament Commentary Philippians, Moody Press, 2001,Chicago, Ill, P 249.

runs to win. All cricket lovers will know how delicate the situation was. Miandad was very careful as he looked around. Could he change the rules by getting some new revelation? No, the rules of the game stayed the same. But he needed to stand with all the knowledge he already had and use it to win the match. The ball came and he batted. He got six runs!

There is an exhortation in Phil. 3:16 to hold on to what we have attained. Every believer needs to live according to the standard he has attained. This is the motivation to go on further into maturity, to learn more, to study more, to pray more and to be disciplined in life. The main area where believers fail is that they do not live a consistent life.

Here are some reminders to living a consistent life:

- Be faithful: Be an honest and sincere steward
- Be obedient: Obey God and don't delay or procrastinate in obeying
- Be diligent: Be sensitive to the voice of God and the promptings of the Holy Spirit
- Be humble: Express your humility, which is costly

Conclusion: I said in the introduction, "Don't waste your years." Many years ago I heard a song in India sung by a lady from North East India. She had a great voice. The song included these lyrics, "Wasted years, wasted years, Oh how foolish, as you wander along a life of sin, turn around turn around to Lord Jesus, you can't go on with a life of wasted years." Don't be stagnant. Forget the past and press on towards the goal.

Chapter 25

What is the Pattern for Your Walk on Earth?

Text: *Philippians 3:17-21* *¹⁷ Brothers, join in imitating me, and keep your eyes on those who walk according to the example you have in us. ¹⁸ For many, of whom I have often told you and now tell you even with tears, walk as enemies of the cross of Christ. ¹⁹ Their end is destruction, their god is their belly, and they glory in their shame, with minds set on earthly things. ²⁰ But our citizenship is in heaven, and from it we await a Savior, the Lord Jesus Christ, ²¹ who will transform our lowly body to be like his glorious body, by the power that enables him even to subject all things to himself.*

Introduction: Let us talk about the pattern for our walk on earth. According to Webster's Dictionary "pattern" means "an example, ideal or a model to be copied." The Greek word 'τυπον' has the same meaning and also includes "standard." Every man creates a pattern by the way he lives. I remember my childhood days when my dad used to take me to our family doctor. This particular doctor had an interesting pattern. He would come into his clinic, sit on his chair and not even look at the patient. His first thing was always to move the things on the table. He would set the table the way he wanted and then turn to look at the patient who had been waiting for a long time. That was his pattern.

What is the Pattern for Your Walk on Earth?

Now what about a walk? What about your life pattern? daily living, reveal your walk on this earth. I remember many things about my father who went to be with the Lord in 1976. His day always began with his morning quiet time. When he prayed, he got on his knees and folded his hands. He did this even in the public prayer meetings. He would get on his knees and fold his hands and then pray. At home after dinner in the evenings he always liked to eat one particular sweet for desert. That was his pattern of life. Look at some kids and notice how they walk. You can immediately point out their parents, either their father or mother, because of the similarities.

Let us now turn our attention to the Scripture to observe the patterns described and choose the right pattern for our walk on earth. There are two different patterns we can live out while on this earth. There is an earthly pattern and a heavenly pattern. If you are already living the right pattern, please go on in living out that pattern. If you have chosen the wrong pattern, please repent and choose the right pattern. Let's look at these two patterns of living.

1. Earthly pattern

Phil. 3:17-19 [17] Brothers, join in imitating me, and keep your eyes on those who walk according to the example you have in us. [18] For many, of whom I have often told you and now tell you even with tears, walk as enemies of the cross of Christ. [19] Their end is destruction, their god is their belly, and they glory in their shame, with minds set on earthly things.

We are talking about an earthly pattern but can you recognize the earthly walk or pattern? Let's look at how we should and should not walk.

First, walk to follow a biblical example not an earthly one. In imitating Christ, you are to follow His example. The English Standard Version says, "Join in imitating me." This appears to be a good translation from the original text. One commentator says that Paul is asking the believers to untidily join in following the example. Is Paul a perfect man? No. Please remember what he said in Philippians 3:12: "Not that I have already obtained this or am already perfect."And consider his words in:

> **Romans 7:18-25** [18] For I know that nothing good dwells in me, that is, in my flesh. For I have the desire to do what is right, but not the ability to carry it out. [19] For I do not do the good I want, but the evil I do not want is what I keep on doing. [20] Now if I do what I do not want, it is no longer I who do it, but sin that dwells within me. [21] So I find it to be a law that when I want to do right, evil lies close at hand. [22] For I delight in the law of God, in my inner being, [23] but I see in my members another law waging war against the law of my mind and making me captive to the law of sin that dwells in my members. [24] Wretched man that I am! Who will deliver me from this body of death? [25] Thanks be to God through Jesus Christ our Lord! So then, I myself serve the law of God with my mind, but with my flesh I serve the law of sin.

Paul was an imperfect man and asked others to imitate him. He knew that he would not be perfect as long as he was on this earth but he knew one thing and that was his deep and sincere commitment to Christ."I have been crucified with Christ. It is no longer I who live, but Christ who lives in me. And the life I now live in the flesh I live by faith in the Son of God, who loved me and gave himself for me" (Gal. 2:20).

There is a further exhortation to observe or watch or keep your eyes on others who walk according to the example set by Paul. Paul was not present physically but Epaphroditus and Timothy were present with the Philippians.

Second, those who walk an earthly pattern walk as enemies of the cross of Christ. Paul was a good shepherd. He cautioned his flock to be careful and often cautioned them about false teachers. There are people around us who are enemies, so watch out.

Acts 20:28-30 [28] Pay careful attention to yourselves and to all the flock, in which the Holy Spirit has made you overseers, to care for the church of God, which he obtained with his own blood. [29] I know that after my departure fierce wolves will come in among you, not sparing the flock; [30] and from among your own selves will arise men speaking twisted things, to draw away the disciples after them.

Paul shed tears because of his concern for others. Commentators refer to the Judaizers as enemies of the cross of Christ. What are the marks of those who are enemies of the cross of Christ? They are:

- People whose end is destruction

Do you know that there is going to be an end to your life? It could be at the time when your heart beats for the last time or at the time when the Lord appears in the air. People who hold on to or teach wrong doctrines have destruction as their end. This is a place of torment – it is hell. "And cast the worthless servant into the outer darkness. In that place there will be weeping and gnashing of teeth" (Matt. 25:30). Any teaching that gives any substitute for the doctrinal truths of soteriology (the doctrine of salvation through Jesus Christ) is wrong teaching. The doctrine of salvation is that we are saved by Christ alone, through faith alone, and by grace alone that leads to redemption.

- People whose god is their belly

People who live by their appetites and do not have a concern for their souls have their belly as their god. Do we have such people today? We need to be warned about these teachers who do not practice true discipleship in their own lives.

- People who glory in their shame

The activities of people who are the enemies of the cross of Christ lead to shame.

- People who set their minds on earthly things

These people do not set their minds on the things that are above. As believers we are told to set our minds on things above. "If then you have been raised with Christ, seek the things that are above, where Christ is, seated at the right hand of God" (Col. 3:1).

2. Heavenly pattern

Phil. 3:20-21 [20] But our citizenship is in heaven, and from it we await a Savior, the Lord Jesus Christ, [21] who will transform our lowly body to be like his glorious body, by the power that enables him even to subject all things to himself.

What does it mean to say that our "citizenship in heaven?" The Bible has clear teachings on heaven. Those people who have been redeemed are citizens of heaven. This helps us to understand what should be our pattern for living. If you belong to heaven, your daily life will show that. Here are some characteristics of a heavenly pattern of life:

- You will store up treasure in heaven
  Matthew 6:20-21 [20] but lay up for yourselves treasures in heaven, where neither moth nor rust destroys and where thieves do not break in and steal. [21] For where your treasure is, there your heart will be also.

- Your security is eternal
  1 Peter 1:3-4 [3] Blessed be the God and Father of our Lord Jesus Christ, who according to His great mercy has caused us to be born again to a living hope through the resurrection of Jesus Christ from the dead, [4] to *obtain* an inheritance *which is* imperishable and undefiled and will not fade away, reserved in heaven for you,

- Your spiritual life on earth is guarded
  Jude 1:24 [24] Now to Him who is able to keep you from stumbling, and to make you stand in the presence of His glory blameless with great joy,

For what is the believer waiting? The believer is waiting for a Savior. In the Old Testament, people were waiting for the first coming of the Lord. The Lord came as a Savior to save people from their sins. He came exactly the way it was told in the Bible. He is now going to come for the second time. It will happen exactly the way it is told in the Scriptures. He is coming!

> **Revelation 22:12-15** [12] "Behold, I am coming soon, bringing my recompense with me, to repay everyone for what he has done. [13] I am the Alpha and the Omega, the

first and the last, the beginning and the end." ¹⁴ Blessed are those who wash their robes, so that they may have the right to the tree of life and that they may enter the city by the gates. ¹⁵ Outside are the dogs and sorcerers and the sexually immoral and murderers and idolaters, and everyone who loves and practices falsehood.

The believer is waiting for the transformation of the human body. The Bible says the believer's body will be changed. The earthly life will be finished. The heavenly life will begin.

1 Corinthians 15:50-53 ⁵⁰ I tell you this, brothers: flesh and blood cannot inherit the kingdom of God, nor does the perishable inherit the imperishable. ⁵¹ Behold! I tell you a mystery. We shall not all sleep, but we shall all be changed, ⁵² in a moment, in the twinkling of an eye, at the last trumpet. For the trumpet will sound, and the dead will be raised imperishable, and we shall be changed. ⁵³ For this perishable body must put on the imperishable, and this mortal body must put on immortality.

The believer is waiting for the subjection of all things to God. You will never have a question on that day as to whether certain things that happened were contrary to the character of God, things such as persecutions, criminal activities or murders. "…putting everything in subjection under his feet. Now in putting everything in subjection to him, he left nothing outside his control. At present, we do not yet see everything in subjection to him" (Heb. 2:8).

Conclusion: What is your pattern for living? Is it an earthly pattern? Or is it a heavenly pattern?

Chapter 26

Exhortation to Admonish

Text: *Philippians 4:1-7 Therefore, my brothers, whom I love and long for, my joy and crown, stand firm thus in the Lord, my beloved. ² I entreat Euodia and I entreat Syntyche to agree in the Lord. ³ Yes, I ask you also, true companion, help these women, who have labored side by side with me in the Gospel together with Clement and the rest of my fellow workers, whose names are in the book of life. ⁴ Rejoice in the Lord always; again I will say, Rejoice. ⁵ Let your reasonableness be known to everyone. The Lord is at hand; ⁶ do not be anxious about anything, but in everything by prayer and supplication with thanksgiving let your requests be made known to God. ⁷ And the peace of God, which surpasses all understanding, will guard your hearts and your minds in Christ Jesus.*

Introduction: We all desire to be encouraged, exhorted and admonished in our lives, don't we? How do you admonish others? Do you exhort or admonish others in the church? Is there a need for the exhortation to admonish others? Some may do so with a "holier than thou" attitude and this is not acceptable in the sight of the Lord. Some may do so with an "I know better" attitude. This also is not proper. Are you accountable if you do not admonish others? This series of questions needs to be understood and obeyed carefully. In this text, the Apostle Paul exhorts us to admonish other believers.

There are lots of expectations for those within the church. Every believer is held responsible. This means he or she is accountable to be a good, faithful, sincere and honest steward. Let us see how we can best be involved in exhorting and admonishing other believers. How are we to do this? There are three keys which will help us as to how, when and whom we should exhort. We are to exhort with affection, exhort for an agreement and exhort regarding the antidote for anxiety. Let's begin with the first key.

1. Exhortation with affection

Phil. 4: 1 Therefore, my brothers, whom I love and long for, my joy and crown, stand firm thus in the Lord, my beloved.

The word "therefore" connects us to the previous text. You'll remember that the previous text gave us a lesson on a "heavenly pattern" and an "earthly pattern" for life. People living an earthly pattern of life live for their stomachs, fulfilling the desires of the flesh. Their end is destruction in hell. We are warned about the false teachers. The Apostle Paul begins his exhortation to the believers by saying, "Therefore." His exhortation is affectionate for several reasons. Take note of, study and follow his example.

Firstly, the Apostle Paul was in love with the believers to whom he wrote. When you think of exhorting others with affection, think of love in biblical terms. Paul taught this in 1 Corinthians and practiced it in his life and writings. This kind of love flows from a man through his attitude, actions and his entire personality. In Greek, Philippians 4:1 reads, Ὥστε, ἀδελφοί μου ἀγαπητοὶ καὶ ἐπιπόθητοι, The actual translation is "beloved." Well, you cannot address somebody as beloved unless you love that person.

Secondly, Paul longed for these believers. This means that he greatly desired or longed for them. In Greek the term refers to "deep pain because of the separation from loved ones."

Thirdly, Paul enjoyed these believers as his joy and crown. Remember that Paul was writing this letter from a prison. In his most difficult times, he had reasons and ways to rejoice and enjoy his life. He referred to the believers of Philippi as his joy and crown. Please look at 1 Corinthians 9:25: "Every athlete exercises self-control in all things. They do it to receive a perishable wreath, but we an imperishable." The word for crown in Greek is στέφανος, meaning, "wreath, crown, prize, reward, gift, reason for pride or boasting." Paul uses the same word here in 1 Thessalonians 2:19: "For what is our hope or joy or crown of boasting before our Lord Jesus at his coming? Is it not you?" Subsequently, Paul admonished them to stand firm in the Lord. Paul only admonished the believers after he expressed all of his affection for them. Is this lacking among believers today? Do you think you need to follow his pattern?

2. Exhortation for an agreement

Phil. 4:2-3 ²I entreat Euodia and I entreat Syntyche to agree in the Lord. ³ Yes, I ask you also, true companion, help these women, who have labored side by side with me in the Gospel together with Clement and the rest of my fellow workers, whose names are in the book of life.

In Paul's exhortation to the believers, Paul went on to talk about two individuals, two ladies. Can you imagine a disagreement between two ladies? Here are two ladies who are perhaps active members in the church. There is not much we

Exhortation to Admonish

know about them but Paul mentioned their names and exhorts them to agree.

To agree "in the Lord," is an expression of a common bond, the same attitude and one cause. A Pauline word φρονέω occurs here. Where else have already seen this word? Please look at Philippians1:7; 2:2 (twice) 5; 3:15, 19 and 4:10 (twice). Paul's not commanding us to agree on everything but on everything that is in the Lord - acceptable to the Lord, suitable in the will of the Lord, complimentary to the plan of God.

- Don't disagree because it is not suiting to your personal convenience.
- Don't disagree because it is not helping you in your personal gain
- Don't disagree because of your personal opinions and views

These women in the church needed help. The Greek word for companion is σύζυγε which is used as a proper name. Suzuge was probably an elder. These ladies are worthy of help because they labored with the Apostle Paul and Clement who was probably another elder. We are reminded here about the book of life (Rev 3:5; Dan 12:1; Mal 3:16; 17 Luke 10:20; Rev 17:8 and 20:12).The names of all the people who are saved and are to be saved are recorded in the Book of Life. Is your name there? Now, who said that the Apostle Paul was anti-women or shunned the ladies? That was not true of Paul.

3. Exhortation of antidote for anxiousness

Phil. 4:4-7 [4] Rejoice in the Lord always; again I will say, Rejoice. [5] Let your reasonableness be known to everyone. The Lord is at hand; [6] do not be anxious about anything, but in everything by prayer and supplication with thanksgiving let your requests be made known to God. ⁷ And the peace of God, which surpasses all understanding, will guard your hearts and your minds in Christ Jesus

We now move to a special and important antidote for anxiety. We all need this. Failure to use this antidote will mean disaster. This antidote is used as a remedy for the sickness of anxiety.

There are seven aspects of Paul's remedy for anxiety.

    i. Rejoice in the Lord always
    ii. Repetitively rejoicing makes us alert
    iii. Reasonableness known to everyone
    iv. Reason: the Lord is near
    v. Requests (of anxiousness) are given to God
    vi. Result that comes from God is peace
    vii. Root is protected

Obeying Paul's command given here through the Apostle Paul is very powerful. It will have a seven-fold affect in your life. Do you want to experience these benefits? His command is very practical and it works. Don't you want it for everyday use? All that you need is faith, a longing and a desire. Let's look at these commands and benefits.

    i) Rejoice in the Lord always

To rejoice is the mark of the believer who lives in victory. "Rejoice in hope, be patient in tribulation, be constant in prayer" (Rom. 12:12). "For the kingdom of God is not a matter of eating and drinking but of righteousness and peace and joy in the Holy Spirit" (Rom. 14:17). "More than that, we rejoice in our sufferings, knowing that suffering produces endurance" (Rom. 5:3).

ii) Repetitively rejoicing makes us alert

2 Corinthians 6:10 as sorrowful, yet always rejoicing; as poor, yet making many rich; as having nothing, yet possessing everything.

iii) Reasonableness known to everyone

The Greek word ἐπιεικής means, "gentle, forbearing, considerate." Let your attitude be gentle and forbearing instead panicking and being frustrated. This is possible in all circumstances through the supernatural power of our God.

iv) Reason: the Lord is near

The word "eggus" means "near" or "close." In context, it refers to space or vicinity. The same word is used in John 3:23 to express physical nearness. "The LORD is near to all who call on him, to all who call on him in truth" (Psa. 145:18).

v) Requests (of anxiousness) are given to God

Matthew 6:27-34 [27] And which of you by being anxious can add a single hour to his span of life? [28] And why are you anxious about clothing? Consider the lilies of the field, how they grow: they neither toil nor spin, [29] yet I tell you, even Solomon in all his glory was not arrayed like one of these. [30] But if God so clothes the grass of the field, which today is alive and tomorrow is thrown into the oven, will he not much more clothe you, O you of little faith? [31] Therefore do not be anxious,

Exhortation to Admonish

saying, 'What shall we eat?' or 'What shall we drink?' or 'What shall we wear?' ³² For the Gentiles seek after all these things, and your heavenly Father knows that you need them all. ³³ But seek first the kingdom of God and his righteousness, and all these things will be added to you. ³⁴ "Therefore do not be anxious about tomorrow, for tomorrow will be anxious for itself. Sufficient for the day is its own trouble.

vi) Result that comes from God is peace

This phrase "peace of God" is found nowhere else in the New Testament.

vii) Root is protected

The word "guard" used here is a military term used for soldiers who guard the city. The New Testament uses this word on four occasions. In one of these instances, it is literally used for guarding of the city (2 Corinthians 11:32).

Chapter 27

Practice What You Have Learned

Text: *Philippians 4:8-9* *[8] Finally, brethren, whatever is true, whatever is honorable, whatever is right, whatever is pure, whatever is lovely, whatever is of good repute, if there is any excellence and if anything worthy of praise, let your mind dwell on these things. [9] The things you have learned and received and heard and seen in me, practice these things; and the God of peace shall be with you.*

Introduction: If I were to ask you, "Have you been practicing what you learned from Sunday's message?" what would be your answer? There are probably some who are scratching their heads to even remember what last Sunday's message was. I was personally reminded at different times of the lessons that were brought before us last Sunday and I claimed the promises given to us in Philippians 4:6-7. If you obey what is taught, you are a blessed person. How do you practice the spiritual teaching of the Apostle Paul? There are two important aspects. These involve focusing your mind and following Paul's pattern. Let's look at these in detail.

1. Focus your mind on issues of relevance

Phil. 4: 8 Finally, brethren, whatever is true, whatever is honorable, whatever is right, whatever is pure, whatever is lovely, whatever is of good repute, if there is any excellence and if anything worthy of praise, let your mind dwell on these things.

The Apostle Paul gives distinctive priorities and admonishes us to focus on them. The word "finally" connects us to a fresh idea that is coming up. It means "in addition to my brothers." Paul challenges the believer to use his or her mind to focus. We see the critical role of one's mind, in terms of our thoughts, intellect, values and desires, in other passages such as:

- Thoughts
  1 Chronicles 22:7 And David said to Solomon, "My son, I had intended to build a house to the name of the LORD my God.

- Intellect
  Hebrews 8:10 For this is the covenant that I will make with the house of Israel After those days, says the Lord: I will put My laws into their minds, And I will write them upon their hearts. And I will be their God, And they shall be My people.

- Values
  Ephesians 4:17 This I say therefore, and affirm together with the Lord, that you walk no longer just as the Gentiles also walk, in the futility of their mind

- Desires
  Ephesians 2:3 Among them we too all formerly lived in the lusts of our flesh, indulging the desires of the flesh and of the mind, and were by nature children of wrath, even as the rest.

With a bit more of an understanding of the mind, on what are we specifically to focus our minds? Paul gives six specific characteristics that are to be true of our thoughts. They are to be:

    i. True
    ii. Honorable
    iii. Right
    iv. Pure
    v. Lovely
    vi. Of good report

All of these qualities must shine in the believer's testimony and be true of his or her thoughts. This is to be the normal and healthy thought-life for every believer. If you don't think on these things, you are a sick person. Let's look at them in more detail.

True: This can only come from God because God is truth.

Honorable: The Greek word means "worthy of respect." Focus on those issues that are worthy of respect. In the Greek world, it was used "to describe what was serious, sublime, dignified, majestic, or august." It is used to describe divinities, law, or the Sabbath.

Right: Don't go by your opinion, especially when you are in anger or troubled. Discipline yourself to focus on what is "right."

Pure: Focus on what is holy and clean. In the Septuagint, the word group refers to cultic purity. In the New Testament, the word occurs only in the Epistles and it means "chaste" (2 Cor. 11:2).

Lovely: This word has the sense of "lovely, pleasing, agreeable, amiable."

Practice What You Have Learned

Of good report – This is a reflection of being gracious and lovable.

You are to focus your mind on the above qualities. Fill your mind with them. Think and meditate on them. Intellectually understand them and desire them to fill your mind. Paul concludes this section with Philippians 4:8: "If there is any excellence and if anything worthy of praise, let your mind dwell on these things."

2. Follow the pattern of Paul

Phil. 1:9 The things you have learned and received and heard and seen in me, practice these things; and the God of peace shall be with you.

Now with our minds filled with these six qualities, we want to follow Paul's example which is promise-based. He instructs us follow the pattern we have learned and received and heard and seen in him, a pattern consistent with the life of Paul.

Let us look at this verse with four questions in mind.

- Do you really understand?
  Are you learning in life? Some people take notes and some people take out their Bibles and seriously study God's Word. Others do not. Some people ask questions, some do not. What about you?

- Are you following Paul's pattern?
  Do you have someone whom you can follow?
  Paul said that whatever the believers learned, received, heard or saw in him, they were to practice these things!

This is a challenge to every believer. A challenge to be transparent in life and a challenge to lead an exemplary life.

- Do you practice?
  This is an exhortation to practice and not just listen. How are you practicing what you have heard and learned each day?

- Do you experience God's peace?
  This is what every believer wants: God's peace.

Conclusion: The only way these qualities can be true of us is discipline and obedience, following the pattern of the Apostle Paul.

Chapter 28

Are You Content?

Text: *Philippians 4:10-13* *¹⁰ But I rejoiced in the Lord greatly, that now at last you have revived your concern for me; indeed, you were concerned before, but you lacked opportunity. ¹¹ Not that I speak from want; for I have learned to be content in whatever circumstances I am. ¹² I know how to get along with humble means, and I also know how to live in prosperity; in any and every circumstance I have learned the secret of being filled and going hungry, both of having abundance and suffering need. ¹³ I can do all things through Him who strengthens me.*

Introduction: The meaning of "content' is "to be independent." It is to be independent of outside need. Many people don't experience this quality of life. They always want more of everything and are never satisfied in life. If you are independent, you would say even in difficult times like when you don't have enough, "I am content." That was the testimony of the Apostle Paul. He had leaned to be content even in times of suffering. Do you want to be content in every circumstance? That is the Christian quality of life. It is a life that pleases God. It is a life that is a blessing to others around you. It is a life that does not experience grumbling, complaining, dissatisfaction and covetousness. Are you content? Let the text transform your life.

Here are two keys to contentment. First, contentment comes through learning and second, contentment comes from the Lord.

1. Contentment is learned

Phil. 4:10-12 [10] But I rejoiced in the Lord greatly, that now at last you have revived your concern for me; indeed, you were concerned *before*, but you lacked opportunity. [11] Not that I speak from want; for I have learned to be content in whatever circumstances I am. [12] I know how to get along with humble means, and I also know how to live in prosperity; in any and every circumstance I have learned the secret of being filled and going hungry, both of having abundance and suffering need

Firstly, the circumstances around you are used to teach you contentment. The Greek word, ἔμαθον is a verb μανθάνω (aor. ἔμαθον, inf. μαθεῖν ; pf. μεμάθηκα) and it means learn, find out, discover, learn by experience or attend a rabbinic school (John 7:15).

Paul's connection with the local church demonstrates the concern of the church for him. This was a matter of great rejoicing for Paul. The adverb μεγαλως means "greatly" or "immensely" and appears nowhere else in the New Testament. Paul's rejoicing was in the Lord. What a blessing it was to have a church that thought of the financial needs of its leaders. The Bible encourages us to do the same. Please look at

> **1 Timothy 5:17-18** [17] Let the elders who rule well be considered worthy of double honor, especially those who work hard at preaching and teaching. [18] For the

Scripture says, "You shall not muzzle the ox while he is threshing," and "The laborer is worthy of his wages."

The Greek word φρονέω means "think, have in mind, care for or be concerned." We must pray that this kind of concern will be found in the church. There should be a proper balance between the expectations of a leader and his expenses. Here is a Christian leader, the Apostle Paul, with various needs, lacking things and not having an abundance. He definitely didn't believe in the Prosperity Gospel. If he did, he would not have been in these kinds of circumstances. Why can't you trust the Prosperity Gospel?

- Because it is inconsistent with the teachings of the Bible
- Because it promotes an imbalanced Christian experience
- Because it promotes an easy life and not a sacrificial life as taught in the Scriptures
- Because it doesn't teach true discipleship
- Because it portrays false spirituality
- Because it promotes a detour route to gain prosperity

The circumstances that Paul faced also included the church lacking the opportunity to help him. Ten years had passed since the first time the Church of Philippi helped Paul. They had had a concern but had no opportunity to give to him. Does this mean that God forgot him? No, these circumstances were helpful to him in order to learn to be content.

Secondly, to be able to be content in every circumstance is a learned skill. This is true even for Christian leaders. Is it human nature to be content? Can contentment be learned? We are exhorted from the example of Israelites that we must learn to be content in every circumstance. Please look at

Are You Content?

1 Corinthians 10:5-11 ⁵ Nevertheless, with most of them God was not well-pleased; for they were laid low in the wilderness. ⁶ Now these things happened as examples for us, that we should not crave evil things, as they also craved. ⁷ And do not be idolaters, as some of them were; as it is written, "The people sat down to eat and drink, and stood up to play." ⁸ Nor let us act immorally, as some of them did, and twenty-three thousand fell in one day. ⁹ Nor let us try the Lord, as some of them did, and were destroyed by the serpents. ¹⁰ Nor grumble, as some of them did, and were destroyed by the destroyer. ¹¹ Now these things happened to them as an example, and they were written for our instruction, upon whom the ends of the ages have come.

2. Contentment comes from the Lord.

Phil. 4:13 I can do all things through Him who strengthens me.

Humanly speaking, it is not possible to be content. We need God's supernatural strength to be content. Do you imagine that God is somewhere "up there" shut in a "holyplace"? If you do, your imagination is absolutely wrong. Please look atPsalm 145:18: "The LORD is near to all who call on him, to all who call on him in truth" and Philippians 4:5: "The Lord is at hand." This means He is close to us because it speaks of vicinity or distance, not time.

"**Prevailing**" in Greek is ἰσχύω and means to be able, can, win over, defeat, be strong, grow strong (Acts 19:20). This is the same word the Lord used in Matthew 9:12 when He said that it is not those who are healthy but those who are sick who need a physician. It indicates strength in the body. The word also means "prevailing" and is used in Acts 19:20 where God says the Word grew mightily and prevailed. It also means "able." Remember, when the disciples caught the fish and they were not able to handle the weight of it? It is the same word used here.

Paul says that he can do all things through Christ. Christ is the one who strengthen us. He is the one who will enable us to do all things. How does this happen? It happens with supernatural power. Supernatural power has no human reasoning or explanation. It is beyond human comprehension.

> **Ephesians 3:16-20** [16] that according to the riches of his glory he may grant you to be strengthened with power through his Spirit in your inner being, [17] so that Christ may dwell in your hearts through faith- that you, being rooted and grounded in love, [18] may have strength to comprehend with all the saints what is the breadth and length and height and depth, [19] and to know the love of Christ that surpasses knowledge, that you may be filled with all the fullness of God. [20] Now to him who is able to do far more abundantly than all that we ask or think, according to the power at work within us.

The Lord's power never fails so we can trust Him at all times. He offers to every believer the ability to live a powerful life at all times. This power also helps every believer to live a life of contentment. "Now there is great gain in godliness with contentment, for we brought nothing into the world, and we cannot take anything out of the world. But if we have food and clothing, with these we will be content" (1 Tim. 6:6-8).

Conclusion: Don't miss out on a life of contentment. You can experience it by learning to be content. You can experience it through the Lord.

Chapter 29

Partnership with God's People

Text: *Philippians 4:14-19* *¹⁴ Yet it was kind of you to share my trouble. ¹⁵ And you Philippians yourselves know that in the beginning of the Gospel, when I left Macedonia, no church entered into partnership with me in giving and receiving, except you only. ¹⁶ Even in Thessalonica you sent me help for my needs once and again. ¹⁷ Not that I seek the gift, but I seek the fruit that increases to your credit. ¹⁸ I have received full payment, and more. I am well supplied, having received from Epaphroditus the gifts you sent, a fragrant offering, a sacrifice acceptable and pleasing to God. ¹⁹ And my God will supply every need of yours according to his riches in glory in Christ Jesus.*

Introduction: The Gospel is to be preached to the whole world. It is the responsibility of every disciple of Christ. Every believer is instructed to be a true disciple of Christ. God's Word gives us a method for preaching the Gospel to the whole world. The local church sends out missionaries and those missionaries go with the call of God. A good example of this is found in the book of Acts chapter 13. The church at Antioch gathered for prayer and sent out missionaries to the field for service. The local church is involved with people in spreading the Gospel. The local church exists to serve God, to bring glory to Him through preaching and to establish His kingdom.

Church history is filled with people who were called to serve Him and the local churches partnered with those missionaries. The names of those who have served are innumerable, but God knows each one.

There are six key aspects or actions that are true of this partnership with God's people. Please remember that this is a partnership with the people of God and not with machinery. You are not partnering with equipment but with the people of God. These are people who are called of God to serve Him.

1. Partner in sharing with the trouble

Phil. 4:14 Yet it was kind of you to share my trouble.

Please note that the Apostle Paul was going through hard circumstances and suffering that is called "trouble' here. The trouble was a need for financial help. He didn't ask or appeal for funds but when they were offered to him, he didn't refuse them either. How could this sharing between the church and this man of God happen? There are three possibilities:

- The local church identified the trouble

    A Christ-centered church looks around to help others in trouble. This is a true picture of the first church in the book of Acts. We read in Acts 2:45: "And they were selling their possessions and belongings and distributing the proceeds to all, as any had need." I personally watched a pastor's wife selling her most expensive sari with its gold threading in order to get money that would help in meeting necessities.

Partnership with God's People

- The local church opened up its resources

    2 Corinthians 8:1-5 [1] We want you to know, brothers, about the grace of God that has been given among the churches of Macedonia, [2] for in a severe test of affliction, their abundance of joy and their extreme poverty have overflowed in a wealth of generosity on their part. [3] For they gave according to their means, as I can testify, and beyond their means, of their own free will, [4] begging us earnestly for the favor of taking part in the relief of the saints- [5] and this, not as we expected, but they gave themselves first to the Lord and then by the will of God to us.

- The local church took responsibility

    The understanding of receiving and giving must be clear in our hearts.

    1 Timothy 5:17-18 [17] Let the elders who rule well be considered worthy of double honor, especially those who work hard at preaching and teaching. [18] For the Scripture says, "You shall not muzzle the ox while he is threshing," and "The laborer is worthy of his wages."

    2. Partner in sharing your treasure

Phil. 4:15 And you Philippians yourselves know that in the beginning of the Gospel, when I left Macedonia, no church entered into partnership with me in giving and receiving, except you only.

This is another area where the church at Philippi is a good example. They expressed their partnership in giving, in sharing their treasure. Paul uses business terms to describe the giving and receiving. Giving and receiving are expenditures and receipts. How did this happen? Let us look at three possible explanations of what Paul meant. First, Paul was called of God and God took care of him through the local church. Secondly, it may mean that the local church was sensitive to God's way of work and was involved in partnership by helping God's servants who were called of Him. Thirdly, it may refer to the local church's partnership for the sake of the Gospel.

3. Partner in sharing at the appropriate time

Phil. 4:16 Even in Thessalonica you sent me help for my needs once and again.

Help is a wonderful means of partnering with God's people. The church in Philippi used this method which still works today. This can happen in any part of the world. You may sit in the West and help people in the East. You can use the resources you have and make them work in India, Pakistan, Sri Lanka, Bangladesh, Myanmar, Tibetor anywhere.

How can this happen? Here are just a few possible ways. First, in your daily devotion, you must be open to what God is saying. Your heart and spirit matter a lot. You must listen with your ears and apply what He says to your heart and spirit. This prepares you to be ready to help others. This brings you out of self-centeredness and into a Christ-centered life. Secondly, identify the needs of others as they are spoken at conferences, mentioned in the magazines, and announced in the churches. Thirdly, implement what you have learned. Open your wallet to help others. Donate generously.

Let me share from my initial experience in Lucknow. During the initial years of my Christian life, there was one thing I was sure of and that was the call of God on my life. With fears and inadequacies, with limitations and lack of experience, I moved forward with internal drive that I knew was the call of God. I landed in Lucknow in January of 1976. To be precise, it was the 15th of the month and I joined the staff of a local church that never gave me any assurance for the future. I was not told about my monthly salary. I was 21 years of age. The EGF (Evangelical Graduate Fellowship)and EU (Evangelical Union)groups in Lucknow were very strong and they constantly invited me to preach but never gave me money (honourarium) for my services. Within a few days of my arrival in Lucknow, the monies I brought with me were gone and I only had a few coins left. I kept these coins for some chai and coffee. I soon began starving for food. One day was gone, the second day came and there was no food. It was either the evening of the second day or the third day that brought two ladies to my room. They were on the staff of a local college. These ladies came to see me because I was sick from hunger, but I never said that I was without food. They showed Christian love and while leaving my room they said that they were going to get me some dinner. I never said no. After a little while they brought two boiled eggs and noodles. That was a great dinner for me. The heart palpitation that I had was gone within no time after eating that delicious food. Well, if you are curious, one of these ladies became my first wife, Mrs. Enid Kumar, now with the Lord. My son feels he is on the top of world when he hears about his mom. Yes, she was the one who brought food to me that night. Though we never had any inclination or thought of getting married at that time, we were married 2 ½ years later. But my story is not over. Month after month, I saw the Lord provide for my needs in amazing ways. How can I forget this? One of my faithful prayer partners and supporters was Mr. Murthy Paul who used to send me 40 rupees at a time. That was an enormous amount for me. With this money, the Lord provided and I was able to help other believers in the church as well.

4. Partner in profitable transactions

Phil. 4:17 Not that I seek the gift, but I seek the fruit that increases to your credit

What does Paul mean that he didn't seek the gift but that there was fruit that increased to their credit? First, we see the unselfish intention of the recipient that contributes to a profitable transaction. The attitude of the recipient is exemplary. Secondly, we see that a profitable transaction increases the credit of the giver. The giver receives a benefit because of his giving.

5. Partner in supplying excess

Phil. 4:18 I have received full payment, and more. I am well supplied, having received from Epaphroditus the gifts you sent, a fragrant offering, a sacrifice acceptable and pleasing to God.

First, the funds given were sufficient. This is a great comfort and relieves stress. Christian leaders and pastors are burdened with stress from people, circumstances and ministry-related issues. They need comfort from the stress of financial pressures and they can have confidence that their needs will be met and the provision will be sufficient. Not every one realizes this. Here was a local church that extended help to the Apostle Paul and it is an example we should all follow.

Second, the funds were acceptable and pleasing to the Lord. Please note the words, "fragrant offering, a sacrifice acceptable and pleasing to God."How is your offering? Does it have a fragrance? Is it a sacrificial offering? This is the meaning of

> **Romans 12:1** ¹Therefore I urge you, brethren, by the mercies of God, to present your bodies a living and holy sacrifice, acceptable to God, which is your spiritual service of worship. ²And do not be conformed to this world, but be transformed by the renewing of your mind, so that you may prove what the will of God is, that which is good and acceptable and perfect.

Does your offering have God's full support? Consider 1 Peter 2:5: "... you also, as living stones, are being built up as a spiritual house for a holy priesthood, to offer up spiritual sacrifices acceptable to God through Jesus Christ." Please also look at Genesis 8:20-21.

6. Partner with a tremendous promise

Phil. 4:19 And my God will supply every need of yours according to his riches in glory in Christ Jesus.

i) God who supplies is tremendous
ii) God supplies according to His riches

Firstly, God is great and it is He who supplies. We must have faith in that God. Many people have a small image of God. They are afraid to ask God for big things. They limit God because of unbelief. They look to their resources and then pray to God. It should be other way round. Look in Christian history and study the lives of the great men of God. By doing this, your prayer life will be revolutionized.

Secondly, God supplies according to His riches, in supernatural ways. He does so in the abundance of His provision. Consider the example we have in the following lengthy passion.

> **2 Kings 7:1-16** But Elisha said, "Hear the word of the LORD: thus says the LORD, Tomorrow about this time a seah of fine flour shall be sold for a shekel, and two seahs of barley for a shekel, at the gate of Samaria." ² Then the captain on whose hand the king leaned said to the man of God, "If the LORD himself should make windows in heaven, could this thing be?" But he said, "You shall see it with your own eyes, but you shall not eat of it." ³ Now there were four men who were lepers at the entrance to the gate. And they said to one another, "Why are we sitting here until we die? ⁴ If we say, 'Let us enter the city,' the famine is in the city, and we shall die there. And if we sit here, we die also. So now come, let us go over to the camp of the Syrians. If they spare our lives we shall live, and if they kill us we shall but die." ⁵ So they arose at twilight to go to the camp of the Syrians. But when they came to the edge of the camp of the Syrians, behold, there was no one there. ⁶ For the Lord had made the army of the Syrians hear the sound of chariots and of horses, the sound of a great army, so that they said to one another, "Behold, the king of Israel has hired against us the kings of the Hittites and the kings of Egypt to come against us." ⁷ So they fled away in the twilight and abandoned their tents, their horses, and their donkeys, leaving the camp as it was, and fled for their lives. ⁸ And when these lepers came to the edge of the camp, they went into a tent and ate and drank, and they carried off silver and gold and clothing and went

and hid them. Then they came back and entered another tent and carried off things from it and went and hid them. ⁹ Then they said to one another, "We are not doing right. This day is a day of good news. If we are silent and wait until the morning light, punishment will overtake us. Now therefore come; let us go and tell the king's household." ¹⁰ So they came and called to the gatekeepers of the city and told them, "We came to the camp of the Syrians, and behold, there was no one to be seen or heard there, nothing but the horses tied and the donkeys tied and the tents as they were." ¹¹ Then the gatekeepers called out, and it was told within the king's household. ¹² And the king rose in the night and said to his servants, "I will tell you what the Syrians have done to us. They know that we are hungry. Therefore they have gone out of the camp to hide themselves in the open country, thinking, 'When they come out of the city, we shall take them alive and get into the city.'" ¹³ And one of his servants said, "Let some men take five of the remaining horses, seeing that those who are left here will fare like the whole multitude of Israel who have already perished. Let us send and see." ¹⁴ So they took two horsemen, and the king sent them after the army of the Syrians, saying, "Go and see." ¹⁵ So they went after them as far as the Jordan, and behold, all the way was littered with garments and equipment that the Syrians had thrown away in their haste. And the messengers returned and told the king. ¹⁶ Then the people went out and plundered the camp of the Syrians. So a seah of fine flour was sold for a shekel, and two seahs of barley for a shekel, according to the word of the LORD.

Conclusion: Do you understand what it means to partner with God's people? Among many important aspects of the Christian life, don't forget this significant aspect regarding partnering with God's people. We are to:

1) Partner in sharing with the trouble
2) Partner in sharing your treasure
3) Partner in sharing at the appropriate time
4) Partner in profitable transactions
5) Partner in supplying excess
6) Partner with a tremendous promise

Chapter 30

Final Words to Radiate God's Glory

Text: *Philippians 4:20-23* ²⁰ *To our God and Father be glory forever and ever. Amen.* ²¹ *Greet every saint in Christ Jesus. The brothers who are with me greet you.* ²² *All the saints greet you, especially those of Caesar's household.* ²³ *The grace of the Lord Jesus Christ be with your spirit.*

Introduction: We have come to the close of the book of Philippians. In the very first lesson we saw that God uses people to establish a church. Paul was obedient to God in going to Philippi.

> **Acts 16:9-12** ⁹ And a vision appeared to Paul in the night: a man of Macedonia was standing there, urging him and saying, "Come over to Macedonia and help us." ¹⁰ And when Paul had seen the vision, immediately we sought to go on into Macedonia, concluding that God had called us to preach the Gospel to them. ¹¹ So, setting sail from Troas, we made a direct voyage to Samothrace, and the following day to Neapolis, ¹² and from there to Philippi, which is a leading city of the district of Macedonia and a Roman colony. We remained in this city some days.

Philippi was founded by a great Macedonian King named Phillip. The city of Philippi was situated in northeastern Greece and was an island. It appears that Jews were few in

Final Words to Radiate God's Glory

number because there was no synagogue in the city. But Paul's visit to this city did not go to waste. Paul didn't do anything in vain because of his vision. This vision gave him a purpose for his life so that his life was not wasted. What does he say, for example to the Thessalonians? "For you yourselves know, brothers, that our coming to you was not in vain" (1 Thess. 2:1).

The Apostle Paul was led by the Lord to see a church planted and to see it grow. Later on Paul wrote this very affectionate epistle. Now it is time to see Paul's conclusion. He uses an ancient method of concluding his epistle.

There are three segments to his final words, words which we should also observe and obey.

1. Give God the glory

Phil. 4:20 To our God and Father be glory forever and ever. Amen.

Does your life radiate His glory? Please remember the previous verse (Phil. 4:19) to refresh your mind as to why we must give God the glory.

If God supplies, He is the source and should, therefore, get the glory. There is cry from the psalmist in Psalms that God should get the glory. "Not to us, O LORD, not to us, but to your name give glory, for the sake of your steadfast love and your faithfulness!"(Psa. 115:1). Failing to give glory to God is dangerous. Please look at

Acts 12:23: "Immediately an angel of the Lord struck him down, because he did not give God the glory, and he was eaten by worms and breathed his last."

What does Paul mean by "glory to God for ever and ever. Amen?"

Revelation 4:9-11 [9] And whenever the living creatures give glory and honor and thanks to him who is seated on the throne, who lives forever and ever, [10] the twenty-four elders fall down before him who is seated on the throne and worship him who lives forever and ever. They cast their crowns before the throne, saying, [11] "Worthy are you, our Lord and God, to receive glory and honor and power, for you created all things, and by your will they existed and were created."

Our God is the only true God and is worthy of glory and honor. That glory is meant for Him alone and is His forever and ever. The word "amen" refers to an agreement that what is said will be done. Do you carefully use the word "amen" in your prayers or do you use it only casually?

2. Greet each other

Phil. 4:21-22 [21] Greet every saint in Christ Jesus. The brothers who are with me greet you. [22] All the saints greet you, especially those of Caesar's household.

The Christian is life all about living in harmony, about healthy relationships and genuine heart connections. There are a lot of people who just give lip service. They are not sincere and honest in their lives. The Word of God exhorts believers to live in light and fellowship with each other.

Paul's greeting is to the "saints" and "brothers." This means it is a Christian greeting and it is to be honest and sincere.

This has to flow from the heart and not just the lips. It comes from a heart that really loves other believers. God wants us to have good relationships with each other. Look at how Paul expresses this in different places: Romans 16:3, 5, 6, 8 and 11; 1 Corinthians 16:20; 2 Corinthians 13:12; 1 Thessalonians 5:26 and Titus 3:15.

Consider the application: How do you greet each other:

- When you meet each other, is there a warm greeting or a cold handshake?
- When you greet each other, does love flow from our heart? Or is it hypocritical?
- Do you even greet each other? Are you happy about it?
- How about when you greet via email and letters?
- Is there holiness in your greetings?

Now Paul goes on to talk about Caesar's household? Who is this? Caesar's household may mean either the kinsfolk of Nero or servants in the palace. It is probable that the reference is to servants in the imperial house. This is a reflection on Paul's preaching and the fact that he preached the Gospel to people everywhere. William Hendriksen says, "…It refers rather to all persons in the emperor's service, whether slaves or freedmen. Such people who had been given employment in the domestic and administrative establishment of the emporer were found not only in Italy but even in the provincees." [1]

    3.   Grace of the Lord Jesus Christ

Phil. 4:23 The grace of the Lord Jesus Christ be with your spirit.

---

1. Hendriksen, William, New Testament Commentary, Galatians, Ephesians, Philippians, Colossians, and Philemon, Baker Books, Grand Rapids, Michigan, 1968,P 212.

Please note the words carefully. It is the grace of the Lord Jesus Christ that we are talking about. Why? This is because only the Lord Jesus Christ is full of grace. "And the Word became flesh and dwelt among us, and we have seen his glory, glory as of the only Son from the Father, full of grace and truth" (John 1:14).

The grace of the Lord Jesus Christ is to be with our spirits. Every human being has a spirit with him. This is the inner man of every person. What happens when the grace of the Lord Jesus Christ is with this spirit?

- You will be graceful in attitude, talk, behavior and approach.
- You will experience the grace of God in your life.
- You will stand in grace and enjoy the life of grace.

How do you view the grace of the LORD? Here are some thoughts about grace. It is:

- God's characteristic:
  Exodus 34:6 The LORD passed before him and proclaimed, "The LORD, the LORD, a God merciful and gracious, slow to anger, and abounding in steadfast love and faithfulness

- God's Gospel:
  Acts 20:24 But I do not account my life of any value nor as precious to myself, if only I may finish my course and the ministry that I received from the Lord Jesus, to testify to the Gospel of the grace of God.

- God's gift:
  Romans 5:15 [15] But the free gift is not like the trespass. For if many died through one man's trespass, much more have the grace of God and the free gift by the grace of that one man Jesus Christ abounded for many.

Conclusion: Give glory to God all of your days on earth and, in eternity, you will do the same. Greet others with a Christian greeting and enjoy the grace of the Lord Jesus Christ which is with our spirit.